# PRAISE FOR FAUST RUGGIERO AND *THE FIX YOUR ANGER HANDBOOK*

"As someone who continues to deal with anxiety, I found *The Fix Your Anxiety Handbook* to be most helpful. 'Anxiety is not who you are, but what you have.' This clarification, and the advice which follows, has given me some very useful tools to acknowledge and separate those anxious feelings when the monster rears its ugly head from the reality of a situation. This book is a valuable tool in the ongoing struggle to stay the course of healthy mental emotions. Stay strong, brothers and sisters!"

—ADAM FERRARA, ACTOR / COMEDIAN

"Faust Ruggiero has it right! The demon or dragon that keeps so many people from attaining their life goals must be slayed and incapacitated. Faust Ruggiero lays out the perfect plan for destroying this beast. This is a wonderful handbook for anybody who wants to move ahead in life."

—DANIEL ROEBUCK, ACTOR

"Faust was a guest on my podcast and everyone loved his concepts on improving life. His book is practical, and would help any person struggling. Thank you, Faust, for the work you do!"

—ELISA JORDANA, RADIO PERSONALITY, MUSICIAN, COMEDY WRITER

"Anxiety can hold us back in what we want to do in life, and Faust Ruggiero's handbook on anxiety is a fantastic tool to overcome those times and help you take back control!"

—TAYLOR DAYNE, SINGER, SONG WRITER

"Faust Ruggiero possesses an abundance of information, and has created program to treat depression that I have never seen before. He has insights into the dynamics of depression, and communicates them in a way that anyone can understand and apply."

—GEORGE NOORY, COAST TO COAST RADIO HOST

# THE FIX YOUR ANGER HANDBOOK

Helping Bring Peace and Sanity
into a Turbulent World

**FAUST RUGGIERO, M.S.**

FYHB PUBLISHING

**Disclaimer:** This book is designed to help you understand the dynamics of anger and provide helpful steps to assist you in your attempts to reduce its impact on your life. Before attempting to incorporate the information and action steps in this book, consult a physician to be sure that you are physically, emotionally, and intellectually capable of including the program in your life.

*Published by:*
**FYHB Publishing**
BANGOR, PA
www.faustruggiero.com

Copyright © 2024 Faust A. Ruggiero

All rights reserved. No part of this publication may be reproduced, stored in a retrieval system, copied in any form or by any means, electronic, mechanical, photocopying, recording or otherwise transmitted without written permission from the publisher.

ISBNs:
Paperback: 978-1-7343830-6-5
Ebook: 978-1-7343830-7-2

Cover and interior design by Gary A. Rosenberg
www.thebookcouple.com

Printed in the United States of America

# Contents

Foreword ................................................................. vii

Introduction ............................................................... 1

## Part One: Foundational Information

1. Who's Angry and Why: Understanding the Process ........... 12
2. Fact and Fiction: The Truth About Anger ..................... 20

## Part Two: The Faces of Anger

3. Verbal Anger: Tongue Lashings with a Purpose ................ 30
4. Fear-Based Anger: The Mask ..................................... 41
5. Frustration-Based Anger: The End of the Rope ................ 49
6. Pain-Based Anger: Internal Attacks ............................ 57
7. Reactive Anger: At the Breaking Point ......................... 66
8. Physiological Anger: It's a Body Thing ........................ 74
9. Righteous Anger: Anger on the High Road ..................... 85
10. Passive-Aggressive Anger: The Secret Punisher .............. 94
11. Volatile Anger: Blowing Your Stack .......................... 103
12. Anger for Profit: Aggressive Control ........................ 112
13. Retaliatory Anger: Reaction with a Plan ..................... 121
14. Addictive Anger: Evolving into Dependence ................. 129
15. Self-Abusive Anger: Anger Turned Inward .................. 137

**Part Three: Building Your Treatment Plan**

16. A Healthy Body: Ground Zero..................................148
17. Healthy Emotions: Raising Your Emotional IQ................159
18. Healthy Mind: Empowering Your Thinking Machine........171
19. Coping Devices: Short-Term Defensive Strategies............181
20. Internal Language: Positive Self Talk..........................190
21. Letting Go: Understanding Forgiveness......................201
22. Getting Help: Trust on a Higher Level.......................211
23. Living With Less Anger: Navigating Your New World......221
24. Good Housekeeping: Maintenance for the Long Haul.......233

Conclusion..................................................................239
References .................................................................240
About the Author.........................................................241

# Foreword

IN A WORLD FILLED WITH CONSTANT STIMULI and pressures, our emotions often take the brunt of the impact. Anger, in particular, can be a formidable force, capable of disrupting relationships, clouding judgment, and hindering personal growth.

Faust Ruggiero's *The Fix Your Anger Handbook* is a beacon of hope for those navigating the tumultuous, judgmental, and scary waters of anger management.

With insight and practical guides such as "Time to Take Action," and "Driving It Home," Faust invites readers on a journey towards understanding, acceptance, and ultimately transformation.

My dear and best friend, Mariel, is often sharing stories of her childhood. In her search for balance and purpose, she peeled back the curtain on the mental health issues of her childhood. She states, "Anger is a secondary emotion to fear. Figure out what your fears are from your childhood. What part of your story are you still hooked into?"

We know that long-term and intense anger has been linked to mental health problems including depression, anxiety, self-harm, and poor physical well-being. We also know that a commitment to becoming healthier physically, mentally and emotionally is your best offer for a better life.

Whether you're seeking to understand your story, tame your temper, mend fractured relationships, or simply find peace within yourself, this handbook offers invaluable guidance and support. Discover the roots of anger from personal triggers to societal influences. Learn how to recognize the manifestations in your life. Faust dives deep into the multiple layers of anger, from pain-based anger to retaliatory anger.

We at the Mariel Hemingway Foundation are often on the hunt for resources to which we can navigate our audience. Faust's expertise helps you discover that the power lies within. Learning how to confront, manage, understand and ultimately overcome your anger are the rewards for having studied his reveals. Embark on this journey of Faust's with a wellness to unlock a life free from the shackles of anger. Working on you is the greatest gift you can offer yourself and your world. As Faust would say, "Onward."

Melissa Yamaguchi
Co-Founder Mariel Hemingway Foundation

# Introduction

**DO YOU WANT TO UNDERSTAND ANGER**, reduce its impact on your life, and eventually free yourself from its paralyzing effects? If so, *The Fix Your Anger Handbook* is for you. This is book four in The Fix Yourself Empowerment Series. It follows the award-winning *The Fix Yourself Handbook* (December 2019), the much-heralded *The Fix Your Anxiety Handbook* (June 2023), and *The Fix Your Depression Handbook* (December 2023).

Consistent with the approach taken in the first three books in the series, the program is presented as a process journey. All the books in The Fix Yourself Empowerment Series are written as journeys. I do this because I want you to understand that life is a journey, and by going slow and understanding the processes associated with it, you can learn how to live a happy and productive life. Also, by presenting the program as a life journey, I can give you a glimpse of what your life can be like during the later stages of the journey—that is, what your life can look like if you stay committed to the advice you read here. The most important point to remember is that being angry is *not* who you are, it is a temporary state you are experiencing.

I describe anger this way to help you understand what is happening to your body, mind, and emotions. I want you to be able to separate yourself from your anger and create a clearer picture of what has happened to you throughout your life as anger becomes a dominant force. When anger takes hold of your life, it overwhelms you, making it difficult to understand what is happening to you. It is extremely important to understand what has caused your anger, what type or types of anger you have, how your anger manifests, and what you can do to reduce the effects of anger in your life.

Each bite-size chapter presents the necessary information to help you understand a specific dynamic about anger. The causes of your anger and how it exerts its influence are discussed, and the precise steps to help you correct the problem are provided as the chapters wind down. I have designed this program so that you can apply the steps to your circumstances. However, as you will see, the problems presented here can be experienced by anyone who suffers from one or more of the various types of anger presented in the book and is looking for a way out of their pain. You are not as different as you think you are, and there *is* a logical way out of your distress.

Consistent with all the books in The Fix Yourself Empowerment Series, *The Fix Your Anger Handbook* is the product of more than thirty years of practical counseling application. I have developed the program, researched it extensively, and used it with great success with my clients. It is a dynamic addition to an existing counseling program, or, if you have difficulty obtaining professional counseling, it can provide you with either a viable alternative or an introduction to that step.

As with all the books in The Fix Yourself Empowerment Series, each chapter opens with a quote that offers a glimpse into the chapter's content. This is followed by the specific processes to employ (see page 12), which will help you do the work to alleviate the problem addressed in the chapter. The processes are to be used as program supports to help you work with all the information and suggestions I make; they are tools you can use as you attempt to implement each step of the program. As you proceed through the program and secure the assistance of a professional counselor and support people to help you reduce your anger, these processes can be included in your discussions with them, and they can help you make the changes I discuss. A few processes—Brutal Honesty, I Over E, Present/Understand/Fix, and Slowing Down Life's Pace—appear in each chapter because they are foundational to the entire program.

There are fifty-two processes in the Process Way of Life program. However, not all of them directly apply to anger. The initial fifty-two processes were included in each chapter of *The Fix Yourself Handbook,* the program's flagship book. In that book, the text is written to address many different problems on the human spectrum; all fifty-two processes were needed to navigate the program presented. In the subsequent books, only the processes that directly apply to the information being discussed in the chapter are used. So don't be concerned if not all the processes are used in this book.

The chapters are short and to the point with direct, concise information. This is the best way to ensure the information is understood, especially when anger can have such a dramatic impact on your life and the lives of those close to you. Since this book can be used as a reference guide, the layout makes it easy to refer back to any chapter if you need a refresher at a later date.

As each chapter concludes, you will find the Time to Take Action sections. Here, I present the exact steps I advise you to take to help you move forward in the program. In everything I teach, I always provide action steps because information without a workable course of action is rarely applicable. These action steps are the fuel that makes the program run. I also provide you with a declaration at the end of each chapter. These affirmations will help you maintain enthusiasm as you continue the program. Each chapter closes with a short introduction to the next chapter.

As you move forward in your life, it will be important to embrace the concept of information-gathering and fact-finding. Correct information always leads to a potential solution. With this in mind, Part One provides foundational knowledge you will need to understand anger, and Part Two discusses different types of anger. It is vital to read these chapters carefully because they will provide you with the information you need to create an efficient plan to address your anger.

In Part Three, you will build your treatment plan to reduce anger's impact on your life. The chapters in this part provide the specific features of a workable plan to help you reduce your anger, as well as the steps to take to formulate that plan and begin your process of recovery from agitating this nemesis. Many people do their best to end their pain and move into a new way of life, but it is unfamiliar ground and they do not have an efficient plan to live there. Therefore, before Part Three concludes, you will learn what you need to do to live in your new world. Finally, you are presented with a viable plan to help you maintain the gains you have made in your recovery from anger.

This book provides you with the initial tools to help you move beyond your anger and will always be available as a reference guide and a long-term ally. Consistent with any program I design and implement, it is not meant to be a quick-fix problem-solver. This is a lifelong program designed to provide the information you need to help move you beyond your anger and live a happy and healthy life without anger causing problems for you. It can also grow and adapt with you as your life continues to change.

If you have read the first three books in The Fix Yourself Empowerment Series, you may notice that in this book, I suggest more involvement with a professional counselor. This is because, with some types of anger, there is a potential to hurt others and/or oneself, often arising from past trauma. This usually demands help on a professional level.

If you are willing to give this program your time and commitment, it will become an invaluable part of your everyday life. You are greater than the anger that has been defining your life. You are great! So get ready to be the master of your destiny. Prepare yourself for a life-changing program. There is a way out of your anger. . . and this is that way! Follow me.

## HOW TO READ THIS BOOK

*The Fix Your Anger Handbook* and the program that supports it is a program for life, and nothing about it should ever move quickly. I advise you to read each chapter slowly, and before you move on to the next chapter, think about what you have read and how you can apply that information. Move to the next chapter when you fully understand what you have read. Then repeat the process with all the chapters.

You may find it best to read each chapter two or three times.

Doing so can provide you with an opportunity to become better acquainted with the information. All of it is designed to provide you with what you need to understand your anger and eventually work through it. It is a good idea to share what you are reading with people you are close to. If you already have a counselor, share it with that person, too.

Anger issues can be difficult to beat, but it is not impossible to do so. Take your time with the program, and apply the action steps in your life. Let others counsel and support you as you take the steps to rid yourself of the anger that has controlled you to live the happy life that has been waiting for you.

Since the experience of anger can have such a profound effect on your ability to understand what you are reading, it is a good idea to share this book with a close friend who can help you interpret and apply the information.

**NOTE:** The sole purpose of the information in this book is to help you understand the dynamics of anger and to suggest some healthy alternatives to help you begin a program that can assist you in reducing your anger and restore sanity to your world. Before starting any program, consult your physician and/or a professional counselor to determine if there is any reason to avoid it or if changes in your medical program need to be made before you start.

## THE PROCESSES—CATEGORIES AND DESCRIPTIONS

| | Process | Description |
|---|---|---|
| 1 | **Personal Inventory** (Alternate and/or related terms: *Internal Focus, Morality*) | The process of focusing our energy inward to allow for the identification of personal strengths and self-understanding, with the goal of understanding our personal principles concerning the distinction between right and wrong. |
| 2 | **Slow and Steady** (Alternate and/or related terms: *Patience, Slowing Down Life's Pace, Incremental Forward Movement*) | The movement away from quick and impulsive behaviors, and into a state of willful tolerance of delay through the deceleration of a lifestyle that leads to poor decisions and internal conflict, with the understanding that only through small, well-planned steps can we create sustained change and improve the quality of our lives. |
| 3 | **Honesty** (Alternate and/or related terms: *Brutal Honesty, Humility, Truth-Telling*) | The process of being absolutely honest with ourselves, even to the point of personal discomfort, and choosing to take a modest view of our own importance for the purposes of opening oneself up to personal growth. |
| 4 | **I Over E** (Intellect over Emotion) (Alternate and/or related terms: *Emotional Control, Fact-Finding, Intelligent Decision-Making*) | Taking the steps necessary to reduce the impact of emotions on our intellectual processes and using our intellect to exhaustively search for the facts in situations that may lead to stress and personal problems, before our emotions have an opportunity to distort them. Cultivating the understanding that knowledge must be applied so it may become a parameter of personal growth. |
| 5 | **Present-Understand-Fix** (Alternate and/or related terms: *Fact-Finding*) | The formula we will use in every chapter to address your problems. We present the problem, we use the facts to understand it, and we take the steps to fix it. |

| 6 | **Surrendering to the Process** (Alternate and/or related terms: Trust, Faith, Belief, Honor, Dignity) | The willingness to have unconditional trust, either in a process or some unknown entity, such as a higher power, and to allow ourselves to become subservient to the processes, so that we can learn to believe in ourselves, knowing we are capable of being the person we want to be. Having learned to do this, we can learn to think, feel, and behave in a fashion that raises our consciousness to higher-order thoughts and feelings and connects us to our innermost spirit. |
|---|---|---|
| 7 | **Effective Communication** (Alternate and/or related terms: Warm Confrontation, Positive Language Reciprocity, Communication, Conflict Resolution, Listening) | Understanding and mastering the art of positive information exchanges. The ability to gather the facts, understand them, place them in an internally cohesive framework and present that framework, intelligently, to others to address problems. Learning to listen to ourselves, and to others, even if the information presents challenges. Understanding that the way we speak to ourselves and to others can set the stage for how we feel about ourselves and how we communicate with others. |
| 8 | **Cleaning House** (Alternate and/or related terms: Life Inventory, Eliminating Toxic People, Housekeeping, Gatekeeping, Boundary-Setting) | The honest review of one's life and those relationships in it. The removal of all people, events, and situations that may cause pain, conflict, confusion, or dysfunction from one's life to make way for positive and functional information and life-enhancing processes, followed by the practice of monitoring who and what may enter our lives thereafter. Setting boundaries regarding who gets in and how close, and learning to defend those boundaries. |

| 9 | **Simplifying Life** (Alternate and/or related terms: Life on Life's Terms, Keeping Life Simple, Life's Natural Flow) | Understanding how to apply life's natural flow in our lives, along with the removal of any irrational, unreasonable expectations, and unnecessary complexity from life to make room for a simpler and more productive way of living. |
|---|---|---|
| 10 | **Living the Journey** (Alternate and/or related terms: Reduction of Destination Living, One-Day-at-a-Time Living, Living in the Moment, Journey Living, Creativity, Passion, Humor) | Releasing one's attachment to a happiness in life that is dependent on one's arrival at specific, magnificent destinations in favor of focusing on the present, with minimum movement back to past people and events, or forward to events which have not yet occurred. The willingness to focus all life energy on our present life and happiness, moment by moment, as life is being lived, and to appreciate the lighter sides of life, thus reducing stress and pain. |
| 11 | **Closure on the Past** (Alternate and/or related terms: *Settling Past Issues, Forgiveness*) | Judiciously reviewing all past situations and events to put closure on them. Once we've done this, we undertake a step-by-step process to understand what we and others have done wrong, to make amends, and allow ourselves to move forward with reduced emotional pain; forgiving ourselves and others who may have hurt us. |
| 12 | **Eyes on the Prize** (Alternate and/or related terms: *Goal-Setting, Time/Energy Management, Learning to Be Comfortable with Being Uncomfortable, Risk-Taking*) | The practice of setting a long-term goal, complete with short-term goals, action steps, and an executable plan to carry them out in a coherent, cohesive, and timely fashion, and then consciously managing our daily clock and applying our energy to healthy modes of thought and behavior. Change, by definition, is unsettling. Temporary, uncomfortable time frames lead to the happiness and fulfillment we seek. That is where understanding and growth live. |

| 13 | **Commitment** (Alternate and/or related terms: *Journey Living, Trust, Faith*) | Enduring dedication. The Process Way of Life takes time, and continuous, unwavering commitment to the program is essential to ensure its success. |
|---|---|---|
| 14 | **Service** (Alternate and/or related terms: *Being in Service*) | The willingness to turn our rewards outward to help serve the needs of others without expectation of notoriety or payback. |
| 15 | **Wisdom** (Alternate and/or related terms: *Sustained Learning, Humility*) | Being committed to remaining an eternal student of life's lessons and positive teaching sources so we can reach our goal of having the experience, knowledge, and good judgment to achieve an understanding of the bigger picture in life and how to apply ourselves there. |
| 16 | **Gratitude** (Alternate and/or related terms: *Trust, Faith, Belief, Honor, Dignity*) | The understanding that we must be grateful for all we are, all we have, and all we can be, and that we must express this in every moment of our lives. |
| 17 | **Maintaining the Program** (Alternate and/or related terms: *System Maintenance, Housekeeping*) | The establishment and maintenance of an internally balanced power source where the intellect, emotions, body, and spirit become one. This power source is always alive and functional, emanating from inside ourselves. |
| 18 | **Internal Balance** | This is the goal of the program. It is the point where our physical, intellectual, emotional, and spiritual attributes operate in a state of enhanced equilibrium. |
| 19 | **Pure Love** | That point in the Process Way of Life where, through internal balance, we allow our new power source to be realized, to wrap itself around all we feel, touch, see, and do. This is love at its purest level. |

PART ONE

◇◇◇◇◇◇◇◇◇

# Foundational Information

**THE FIRST TWO CHAPTERS OF THE BOOK** will provide you with the information you need to begin to understand what anger is, the different types of anger, and how anger affects your life. This is general information. In the chapters that follow, the information about the different types of anger will be presented in greater detail.

# CHAPTER 1

# Who's Angry and Why: Understanding the Process

*Understanding that no one is free from anger is the first step in learning how to live an anger-free life.*

**PROCESSES TO EMPLOY:** Brutal Honesty, I Over E, Present/Understand/Fix, Slowing Down Life's Pace, Internal Focus, Fact-Finding

MOST OF US EXPERIENCE ANGER and or angry outbursts on occasion. For some of us, anger seems to be a routine part of our lives, while for others, it can be a more isolated reaction to something that triggers an emotional response. Sometimes, the anger is quickly expressed and seems to dissipate just as quickly. Other times, it can have a longer shelf life and find its way into other parts of our lives.

Anger does not seem to be relegated to a specific segment of the population. It can affect any age, race, gender, intellectual level, and social class. You can be hotheaded or even-tempered. You can be a scholar or have limited education. You can be rich or poor. You can be successful or fail at everything you do. Anger has the power to turn a brilliant intellect into a raging lunatic. Anger doesn't care who you are, and it does not discriminate. It can infiltrate even the most tranquil minds, and it can lay waste to the most loving relationships.

Before we move forward, I will offer a working definition of "anger," as I am discussing it in this book. Anger is often described as a feeling of strong annoyance, displeasure, or hostility. This certainly describes what we see or feel as anger begins to make its way into our lives. However, there is quite a bit more involved with anger that lingers and interferes with our happiness. For this book, I am defining "anger" as *an aggressive physical, emotional, and intellectual strategy or response to people, places, and things that can negatively impact our lives and the lives of those close to us.*

In Part Two, I'll discuss the faces of anger. These are the various types of anger people experience. For some, it may be one particular type of anger that affects their lives. For others, there may be two or more that find their way into situations that affect the way they think, feel, and behave. No two people experience anger exactly the same way. To help set the stage for the information I present as we continue, it is important to have a general understanding of how anger develops, how it affects one's thinking, and how it is expressed externally to other people and in various situations. Also, sometimes, when you witness an injustice (a person roughhousing a child for instance), the anger they feel serves the purpose of getting the perpetrator to stop. There are efficient ways to express anger, even in these circumstances, as you shall soon see.

All three attributes (physical, emotional, and intellectual) are always involved in the feeling and expression of anger. The severity of involvement of each of the attributes can depend upon the person experiencing the anger, the people involved in the experience, the place the experience is developing, the coping skills that person has, and other important personal dynamics that may play a role in defining a person's life. This explains why some people process anger so much differently than others. Let's look at the ways anger can affect you physically, emotionally, and intellectually.

## ANGER'S PHYSICAL EFFECTS

It is important to discuss anger's effect on the body first because it can drastically change the way the body operates and because so much about anger can be expressed in physical terms. This does not mean that anger will only be expressed through angry outbursts. The concern is that anger changes the way the body works, activating the fight or flight response, and significantly raising adrenaline, causing a rapid heartbeat, muscle contractions, and to varying degrees, affecting the different systems in the body—the cardiovascular system, digestive system, endocrine system, integumentary system, lymphatic system, muscular system, nervous system, reproductive system, respiratory system, skeletal system, and the urinary system.

Anger can affect eating habits, digestion and expulsion, sleep, and daily relaxation. It affects blood pressure and respiratory rates, and since it significantly increases pressure throughout the body, its long-term effects can range from mild to permanently damaging. Since anger causes such a drastic change in the way the human body works, it is important to understand how these physical changes can lead to what will happen emotionally and intellectually as distressing situations develop.

If you think about a time when you were angry, you were likely focusing on what you were thinking and feeling about what happened. If you were to tune in to your body, you would note that it was not calm and you were feeling some of the effects mentioned previously. Now, imagine the same events occurring, but your body does *not* react to what you are thinking and feeling. You might have more control over how you ultimately react.

It is essential to understand the physical impact of anger. As we proceed, you will learn not only how anger affects your body but also what you can do to strengthen your body to resist the escalation of anger. Also, becoming healthier and more proactive can shorten how long anger affects you, reducing the magnitude of its physical effects and providing you with more control over how you respond. I will discuss more about how a healthy body can help you in your fight against anger in Chapter 16.

## ANGER'S EMOTIONAL EFFECTS

Neurophysiological changes (physical changes in the nervous system) are associated with thoughts, feelings, and behavioral responses that lead to a person feeling pleasure or displeasure. As I stressed in the first three books in this series, your nervous system is involved in everything you do. Your brain (which controls your thoughts and emotions) and your body are intricately connected. The communication system between your body and brain is necessary for you to continue living and has much to say about the way you live your life.

We all have emotions, and we all express them in ways that are specific to how our bodies work and the way we think. They are, in their truest form, an expression of how we feel about what we are thinking and experiencing. However, they are also expressed in response to what our bodies are experiencing. Anger can quickly engage the fight-or-flight response. Anger is processed in our brains, and carried through the body via our nervous system. Since anger is often an emotional response that is designed to either engage us in battle or quickly remove us from the battlefield, it can interfere with our brain's ability to interpret the information we need which will allow us to make good decisions regarding how we are going to respond to anger-provoking situations. This is because neurological energy is being directed to physical action and more closely connected to our emotions, rather than our intellectual processing center, our brain.

Recall a time when you became very angry at someone; you were faced with a quick decision to either stay and fight or remove yourself from the situation. The fight-or-flight response is not a time-consuming evaluation of perceived danger as it is occurring; the response is quick and designed to put an end to what may be perceived as a threatening situation. In situations of profound anger, the brain interprets what is occurring as a threat and must quickly react at a primal level, helping you decide whether to battle the adversary or flee from the threat. In either case, your emotions are involved. You run away because you fear what may be happening. As one of our most intrinsic emotional responses, fear tells the brain that something serious could happen, and using this emotion, you quickly escape from the threat. On the other hand, anger is often interpreted as the antithesis of fear. It can feel like confidence or courage and can keep you in a threatening situation, prompting you to engage in battle.

Even when there is no imminent danger, emotions can find their way into the discourse. The fight-or-flight response is typically engaged as the result of a harmful situation, but that harm does *not* have to be physical. It may also be the perceived potential for emotional damage. The possibility of emotional damage can also engage the fight-or-flight response, and, again, we will either quickly leave the situation or engage in a battle to protect our emotions.

So, emotions do play an important part in the way we deal with threatening and/or anger-provoking situations. Since emotions are closely attached to our primal instincts, when they are expressed in angry situations, they are often overreactive and short on realistic information. As a result, they can make a difficult situation worse and instigate an entirely new set of anger-provoking circumstances.

In *The Fix Yourself Handbook*, I discuss in detail how to allow your intellect enough time to keep your emotions from influencing you to make decisions that are not always in your best interest. As you will learn, involving your intellect in precarious situations carries the potential for more intelligent decisions while helping you avoid the backlash that can result from angry outbursts.

## ANGER'S INTELLECTUAL EFFECTS

When an individual's ability to reason and place factual information in an objective and applicable framework is working efficiently, we are more likely to see clarity of thought, goal-oriented thinking, good decision-making, and plans that embrace the bigger picture. The process of memory functions more efficiently, thought is ordered, and decisions regarding how to respond to other people and life circumstances are rational and well-conceived.

During these periods, the amount of energy being directed to intellectual pursuits like fact-finding, organization of information, and plan formulation can be maximized. When a person's mind is clear and focused, the mind appraises situations efficiently, does not overreact to what is occurring, receives and organizes information correctly, and makes efficient and intelligent decisions regarding what steps to take to address the situation based on the information it has collected and organized.

That said, there will always be people and situations that

challenge us regarding our ability to efficiently perceive what is occurring and act on it appropriately. Unless we are suffering from some kind of intellectual processing disorder or have experienced traumatic brain injury, we typically possess the faculties that are necessary to understand information correctly and act on it appropriately. However, when the accelerated pace of our bodies and/or overriding emotion makes its way into intellectual functioning, our neurological operating system can come under attack.

I have always described the impact of our emotions on our behavior by using the analogy of a computer's operating system. The operating system is designed to run according to algorithms that direct the computer's internal programming. As long as there is nothing to infect the system like a virus or malware, the computer runs efficiently. However, if it becomes infected by one of these antagonists, its efficiency is sharply reduced or stopped altogether. When they are strong enough, emotions can do to our brains what a virus does to a computer. When our emotions become strong enough to override our mind's intellectual programming, we experience difficulties in our ability to understand and interpret information.

The human brain is a marvelous machine. In addition to controlling or at least being involved in every bodily function, it perceives and interprets information coming both from our senses and our internal thought processes. It also is involved in our emotions since emotions are processed in our brains. So, when we become angry, there is a shift in the way our body functions and the strength of our emotions. Now, energy is being diverted away from our intellectual processes and is supporting the in-the-moment fight-or-flight response.

This marvelous machine can also create anger, as you will see in Chapter 12. Just because the brain's efficiency to interpret information is compromised by anger's emotional and physical effects does not mean that it will not understand what is happening when we are angry. Our brain is tasked with the responsibility to use the information available to it to our advantage. It *does* understand that we are angry and may even understand where the anger is coming from. Over time, our brains can also begin to understand how we can use anger *before* a threatening situation develops. Our brain can understand that anger can be used for profit—that is, not only to help us avoid experiencing what we don't want but also to help us get what we *do* want. It possesses the knowledge that it can control people and situations by using anger. Now, anger is no longer a response but a preconceived agenda.

When the brain gets to the point where it understands how to use anger to manipulate and gain an advantage, it can work synergistically with our body and our emotions. Anger now has become a tool, one that can be called upon to punish others, for strategic planning, and/or to help us control our own lives and those of others. Our sophisticated thinking machine is always learning, and it can learn to use anger to our advantage. When this happens, we begin to rely on this manipulative tool to the point where it can become difficult to operate in our daily lives without using it routinely. There's more about addictive anger in Chapter 14.

## KEY TAKEAWAYS

Keep these three important takeaways in mind as you move forward:

First, *anyone can become angry*, even people who seem to be even-tempered and tranquil. Sometimes, anger is expressed overtly such as with acts of destruction and verbal assaults, and other times, it can be a covert form of anger, such as withholding affection or using the silent treatment.

Second, *commonly thought of as an emotion, anger is a combination of physical, emotional, and intellectual processes*. Sometimes one attribute plays a dominant role, and other times there may be a combined attribute effort. The role of all three attributes are discussed in detail as we proceed.

When it comes to understanding anger, the third and most important point is to move away from the simplified belief that anger is simply an emotion that may cause us to lose control, depending on the severity of the situation. *Anger is much more than an emotional response to something we experience or perceive.* There is far more involved, as you will learn in Chapter 2.

**TIME TO TAKE ACTION**

1. Make a list of the times you became angry during the last month and describe what you did during those times. This will help you understand how your anger develops and how you express it.

2. Try to determine how your anger progresses. Knowing where it starts physically, emotionally, or intellectually helps you understand what you need to do to address it.

3. Try to determine if there are triggers in your life that cause you to respond with anger. Don't try to do anything with your anger just yet. You will learn to address your anger in Part Three.

 **DRIVING IT HOME**

All of us can experience anger at one time or another, especially in threatening situations. The most important way to address anger is to understand what causes it and how it manifests—that is, how it progresses in your life. Anger is rarely a one-dimensional enterprise. It affects your body, your emotions, and your intellectual processing. It can quickly initiate the fight-or-flight response and, as a result, give you little time to process what is occurring. Learning to understand your anger is the first step in understanding the role it plays in your life and in laying the groundwork to move into a more peaceful way of living. Part Two provides information to help you identify the type of anger you tend to use most often.

CHAPTER 2

# Fact and Fiction: The Truth About Anger

*Anger is a cancer that infiltrates every part of your life. The faster you understand the facts about this nagging nemesis, the faster you can feel good about yourself and your world.*

**PROCESSES TO EMPLOY:** Brutal Honesty, I Over E, Present/Understand/Fix, Slowing Down Life's Pace, Internal Focus, Fact-Finding

**NOTHING CAN HELP YOU FORMULATE A PLAN** to move past your anger better than acquiring the facts about this potentially life-wrecking way of thinking and behaving. Anger is so commonly perceived as an emotional response to a person or situation that we find displeasing, threatening, or challenging in some way. Angry responses such as arguing, threatening, and physical outbursts are the way anger is often expressed, but they do not define anger.

As mentioned in Chapter 1, it is important to consider the physical, intellectual, and emotional ways anger develops and is finally expressed. However, it is important to first remove some of the misconceptions attached to anger. This will help you establish an understanding of anger based on the facts. It is essential to develop a foundational framework to build upon before we proceed to the more involved parts of the program.

# ANGER: FACTS AND FICTION

**FICTION**: Anger is a mental health problem.

**FACT**: Occasionally feeling angry is not a mental health problem. Even the healthiest people experience periods of anger. It may have its etiology in a physical problem, it could be a habitual way of thinking and behaving, or it may be a quick-tempered emotional response. While it is accurate to say that controlling anger will benefit one's mental health, anger, in and of itself, is not a mental health condition.

**FICTION**: An angry person will always be an angry person.

**FACT**: The human mind possesses the ability to change the way it operates and it has the capacity to learn. Also, any physical problems that may either instigate or exacerbate anger can be addressed. Anger does *not* have to be a dominant condition in one's life with no way out.

**FICTION**: Anger is the same as aggression.

**FACT**: One does not have to be aggressive when one feels angry. As stated in Chapter 1, you do not need to fight in anger-provoking situations. A person often has the option of removing themselves from a perceived threat. Aggression is one of the potential responses to anger, but it is not the only one that is available.

**FICTION**: Anger management doesn't work.

**FACT**: Anger-management techniques have been highly successful in helping people identify what type of anger they have and where it is coming from. It also provides people with coping mechanisms to help them deal with their anger and therapeutic methods to help them change the way they respond to anger-provoking situations.

**FICTION**: Anger is not always abusive.

**FACT**: The truth of the matter is that anger is always abusive in one way or another unless it engages to assist another person such as protecting a child from an abuser. It doesn't matter whether it is verbal or physical abuse. It doesn't matter whether it is directed toward another individual or to oneself. Anger causes pain regardless of how it is expressed, even if it lasts for only a few moments.

**FICTION**: Anger is easy to spot.

**FACT**: Not all anger has the definable parameters we see in overt expressions of physical and verbal attacks. Sometimes anger is subtle and passive, and sometimes it is sneaky, an outgrowth of a strategic agenda. This is discussed in greater detail as we proceed.

**FICTION**: Anger is all in your head.

**FACT**: As you learned in Chapter 1, anger is not purely an intellectual enterprise. It is typically the combination of what your body is feeling, what your mind is thinking, and what you are experiencing emotionally.

**FICTION**: Venting your anger releases it.

**FACT**: For some people, venting anger can help them minimize the effects of the physical, emotional, and intellectual symptoms but usually only for a short period. Venting is a short-term fix that can provide some immediate relief, but it also carries with it the potential for additional anger and, at times, collateral damage, especially when one is venting to another person. There is venting, but there can also be a response to the venting.

**FICTION**: Anger is purely an emotion.

**FACT**: Anger is not purely an emotion. This is one of the misconceptions, and it has led to incomplete methods of treating it. Anger is often classified as an emotion because there is so much emotional expression when it occurs. There is more to it as we saw in Chapter 1. It is more difficult to control one's anger if you focus only on one attribute. Anger is experienced on the emotional level, but also the intellectual and physical levels.

**FICTION**: Anger automatically leads to aggression.

**FACT**: As you will see in Part Two, some types of anger are not expressed by using aggression. As the human mind begins to understand aggression, its intellectual capacity regarding the dynamics of anger is increased and it learns how to use it. Like anything else in our lives, our brain does what can to understand what is happening to us and how we can use some of its components to our advantage. This is referred to as habit formation and is discussed in detail in the first three books in this series.

**FICTION**: Ignoring your anger will always make it go away.

**FACT**: This is seldom the case. You may push something aside or compartmentalize it intellectually, which may fool you into believing that the matter has been resolved. In incidences of mild anger, ignoring it has merit. However, ignoring anything that has enough power to affect us physically, emotionally, and intellectually magnifies the potential for increased severity and responses that can be damaging to oneself and others.

**FICTION**: Men are angrier than women.

**FACT**: The truth of the matter is that men tend to express anger differently than women. Both men and women experience anger, and it can have a profound effect on their lives. Testosterone can provoke angry episodes, and men tend to be more demonstrative with their anger, but that does not mean that women don't get angry as often as their male counterparts. An important note is related to the hormonal differences between men and women. Since testosterone can be a catalyst for overt anger, men tend to respond angrier and faster. Women tend to have a slower boiling point since progesterone and estrogen don't have the same anger-provoking properties as testosterone. However, women experience hormonal imbalances more often than men. This can lead to periods of intolerance, increased stress, and angry responses and behaviors.

**FICTION**: Suppressing anger is better than expressing it.

**FACT**: Anytime we are thinking or feeling something that is causing us discomfort, it is a good idea to do what is necessary to put the event in a coherent perspective and, if possible, do something about it. Suppressing anger keeps it internal, often with little or no way to resolve the problem. One does not need to vent angrily, but it does make sense to communicate what you are thinking and feeling, either to the person who is causing the problem for you or with someone who can help you organize your thoughts and develop a plan to address what has occurred.

**FICTION**: Anger is inherited.

**FACT**: Some evidence suggests anger can be linked to our genetic makeup. Human beings are the product of their parents' genetic codes and can be predisposed to develop certain health concerns, as well as intellectual and emotional processing similarities. However, there is also the interaction between our genetic programming and our environment. Evidence also suggests that children brought up in angry households learn angry tactics, further complicating genetic programming. So, some of anger's environmental programming may be imprinted at birth, but your brain is a learning machine, and nothing about anger is unchangeable.

**FICTION**: Anger cannot be controlled.

**FACT**: A person can certainly learn to control their anger. It is a process of defining the anger, where it is coming from, and understanding what to do with it. Understanding how anger is affecting you personally sets the stage for the development of a plan to reduce its impact on your life.

**FICTION**: People, places, and things make you angry.

**FACT**: People and events can cause you to become angry. The real way to express this is that *you are responding with anger* to people, places, and things. No one has so much power over you that they can make you feel angry. Other people do not control what you think or do. You may not like what you were experiencing, but you do have options regarding what you do about it. This will become more apparent as you proceed through this book.

## UNDERSTANDING IT AND LEARNING WHAT TO DO WITH IT

Nothing sets the table for success more efficiently than understanding the facts relative to any endeavor. So much of what we previously believed about anger is based on antiquated one-dimensional principles that led to the belief that it could not be successfully treated. We all have physical, emotional, and intellectual attributes, and we all can experience anger as a function of the way it is processed by these attributes.

All too often, we become protective about something we feel sheds negative light on who we think we are and what we want others to think about us. No one wants to be thought of as an angry person. So, we do our best to protect ourselves from an unwanted label. As soon as we understand that everyone experiences anger and that we are not abnormal if we get angry, we begin the process of learning to live with it and work our way through it. Anger is like any other problem that finds its way into our lives. We can deny its existence, but we will still experience its negative effects as we express our anger in situations that could have been addressed without it.

Understanding that you can become angry and that anger may be causing you to live a life that is not quite as happy as it can be isn't something to be embarrassed about. It is not something to hide. It is simply another part of your life to understand and learn how to change. One of the most debilitating parts of anger is to become angry about being angry and to feel as though you will never be free of it.

Be willing to acquire the information you need to understand what is happening to you when you become angry, where it is coming from, and how you are going to change it. The bottom line is simple: You will either reduce your anger or it will continue to affect your life—and not always for the best.

 **TIME TO TAKE ACTION**

1. Make a commitment to acquire as much information as you can about anger and how it is affecting your life.

2. Reread the section about fact and fiction regarding anger. Make a list of the important facts about anger as you think they currently pertain to you. This will help you understand how it is affecting you.

3. Before moving on to Part Two, list the ways you think anger is affecting your life. Pay special attention to what you do when you get angry and the effect it has on you and others. Once again, don't do anything with the information you are receiving just yet. We will take these steps as we progress in the program.

 **DRIVING IT HOME**

Everyone gets angry, and that's real. When you attempt to hide your anger, you are hiding it from other people, who also get angry. Start with a blank slate regarding what effect you think anger is having in your life. Throw out the old misconceptions about what anger is and where it comes from. From this moment on, surrender to the notion that your humanity includes an angry component in its design. It is a lot easier to move forward with your plan to reduce anger in your life if you are not trying to defend yourself and refuse to admit that it is there. Having anger is not your problem; not knowing what to do with it is. Anger is very treatable, and becoming educated about it is the first step you need to take to reduce its impact on your life.

**YOUR DECLARATION IS:** *I will work with the facts, and I will learn how to reduce anger's impact on my life.*

 **ONWARD**

There are many different types of anger, and it is important to understand which of them play a role in the way you live your life. I will continue your anger education with the faces of anger. The first chapter in Part Two focuses on verbal anger and how it affects you and the person you attack with your angry words.

# PART TWO

# The Faces of Anger

**IN PART TWO, I DISCUSS AND EXAMINE** the various types of anger, how they develop, what sustains them, and how they manifest and can affect your life. The list is not exhaustive, but it does present the more prevalent types of anger and how and why we tend to use them in our lives. I will be starting with verbal anger.

CHAPTER 3

# Verbal Anger: Tongue Lashings with a Purpose

*The target of verbal anger is an adversary's intellectual/emotional jugular. In the end, however, it is nothing more than a representation of our own insecurities.*

**PROCESSES TO EMPLOY:** Brutal Honesty, I Over E, Present/Understand/Fix, Slowing Down Life's Pace, Internal Focus, Fact-Finding, Warm Confrontation, Communication, Boundary Setting, Living in the Moment, Settling Past Issues

**MOST OF US HAVE EITHER DIRECTED** our verbal assaults on other people or have been victimized by their verbal onslaughts. The title of this chapter seems to suggest that verbal attacks must use explosive language, backed by fierce emotion and designed to take the legs out from under their victims. This isn't always the case. Not all verbal assaults have these characteristics. Sometimes, the assaults are hidden in tongue-in-cheek comments, sinister humor, agenda-loaded gossip, and degrading putdowns. Expressions of verbal anger are typically used for the following reasons:

➤ They are designed to hurt or get even with others in some fashion.

➤ They are used as a way to protect oneself from the possibility of being hurt by another.

➤ They are used to gain an advantage over another person.

- They can relieve the pressure that comes from holding anger in, especially when another person is the object of that anger.
- They are overt representations of one's internal thought processes.
- They can be used to mask fear in some situations.

Sometimes verbal anger is automatic. It can be the default way a person responds in situations that produce anxiety, frustration, or anger. When this happens, there is usually very little thought being applied to what is being said. Some people's anger accelerates quickly, and for those people, firing back verbally can provide a quick release of negative energy. It also carries the potential of setting the other person straight by letting them know you are not happy with what they did, or how they may have hurt you or caused you some sort of discomfort.

Other times, verbal assaults are expressed without a triggering episode. In these instances, rather than accelerating to a quick boiling point, the person has been simmering for a while. Typically, those who gradually build emotion arrive at a point where they can no longer hold their anger in. Then, everything on their minds is expressed, quickly and in no uncertain terms. I'm going to break down each of the six expressions of verbal anger listed above to help you understand how and why they are used.

## TO HURT OR GET EVEN

It is not uncommon to experience times when you feel someone has insulted you, hurt you, or has done something that makes you feel like you are at a disadvantage. Sometimes, it is difficult to walk away from someone who insults you but behaves as though nothing has happened. Although we are usually taught to take the high road, during these times, especially if they occur repeatedly, evening the playing field feels warranted. You may know that lashing out is not the right thing to do, but sometimes that just doesn't matter. Sometimes, you just want to make the pain go away, and taking the high road doesn't seem to be working.

When getting even with someone is a response to what they have done, it may be expressed on the spot or you might take some time to think about how you want to hurt that person. Quick responses usually include a returned verbal assault that might embarrass the other person or instill fear in them. It is typically an emotional reaction with little intellectual planning. Something happens, your emotions go from zero to sixty in a second, and you fire back. This is a verbal example of the fight-or-flight response, where you choose to stand your ground and let the other person have a proverbial piece of your mind. Other times, you may choose to walk away, think about what happened, and plan how you will respond the next time. In each of these cases, you are defending yourself—at least in your mind.

There are also times when verbal assaults might come from inside you. You may be living an angry lifestyle with a low tolerance for others. Sometimes, evening the playing field is about diverting conscious energy away from your insecurities. At these times, you may lash out at someone just because you feel threatened emotionally, even though they haven't done anything to you. Angry people think angry thoughts. They don't always need an external triggering event or another person to express anger. Our behavior is very often an expression of what we are thinking. So, if you are typically thinking angry thoughts, you are more inclined to express those thoughts without provocation.

In any situation where you feel as though you want to verbally undress another person, it is a good idea to pause and think about where this behavior is coming from. If you have already verbally attacked them, go back, review the situation when you are feeling less emotional, and, once again, look at why this is happening. No one has so much control over you that you must respond with anger. There will be times when you feel justified in letting someone have a piece of your mind. The question is, how long do you want to continue to live with anger and find yourself in situations where verbal anger needs to be expressed?

It is always a good idea to take a step back and think about the way you want your life to be lived. If hot debates, heated arguments, and angry thoughts that turn into angry verbal assaults are not the way you want to live, there are other ways to address these situations. So, the advice here is to routinely examine the way you are thinking when it comes to anger. This can tell you what options are available to you in situations that can cause you to become angry.

Verbal anger isn't always overtly expressed. Sometimes, verbal anger is expressed in your mind, which is where everything starts. Examining the way you think and how often your thoughts are angry is a great way to start moving past an internal world inundated by angry thoughts. This will help you understand what is happening in your mind *before* it makes its way to the external world and to those who live there.

## TO PROTECT ONESELF FROM THE POSSIBILITY OF BEING HURT

The keyword here is "possibility." The traditional understanding of how anger works is that when something happens, you become angry, and you respond with some form of aggressive outburst. The truth of the matter is that nothing must happen for you to become angry. As I mentioned previously, it can start in your mind. Part of your brain's survival mechanism is to anticipate the possibility that something threatening or potentially harmful to you may occur. So the brain stays in a kind of security mode, putting a defensive force field around you and providing you with the necessary weaponry to fend off any attacker.

Remember, verbal anger does not have to be expressed in response to something that has happened. Fearful of the possibility of a threat, your brain can launch protective scouts, verbal warnings that let others know it is not a good idea to mess with you. Most of us have friends or family members who use verbal messages to let us know they are willing to wage war, if necessary if we decide to do anything that could put them at risk. Typically, they do not initiate their verbal defense system in an all-out angry outburst. Instead, their verbal presentation can be just a bit aggressive. It lets you know, in no uncertain terms, that there are lines you should not cross.

An example of protective verbal anger is a person who can be sarcastic and confrontational. This is their default presentation, and as a result, others in their company choose not to push past these warnings. People who use this protective mechanism are usually people who are dealing with some form of past trauma or abuse, as they perceive it. Fearful that such an episode may be repeated, they launch an offensive before any battle begins. So, in this case, verbal anger is not expressed in response to any person or triggering event; rather, the person has likely not yet come to terms with a past dramatic or painful situation. The anger being expressed in this case comes from internal sources, but it is being expressed externally even before an event begins. Since the person using this type of anger has not reconciled the events of the past, anger is the driving source behind their verbal protection. If they had reconciled the past event, they could still use language to address a perceived threat, but it would not need to come from angry motivators. This would be a much healthier way to address the situation.

## TO GAIN AN ADVANTAGE

No one likes to feel as though they are second best or that they might find themselves either at a disadvantage to someone else or facing the possibility of being hurt by them. Fear and insecurity are extremely potent motivators for anger. All of us have our insecurities, some of which are more intense, and others less potent. No one likes to feel insecure or be at someone else's mercy. Once again, the brain goes into protection mode.

In yet another example of getting ahead of the potential to be hurt by someone, verbal anger can be used to help you feel as though you are on equal footing with other people. If other people possess the potential to take advantage of you, you will do what it takes to verbally hold them at bay or even intimidate them with the language you are prepared to use; this may convince them to refrain from imposing their will on you.

The perception of an attack, however, is not the only time verbal anger can be used to gain an advantage over someone else.

Sometimes, the other person might purposefully or inadvertently do or say something to put you in a position where you feel subordinate. An angry verbal response might quickly subdue your oppressor. For example, perhaps you have a friend who typically uses words or actions to gain an advantage over you. Perceiving that this may happen, you may strike the first verbal blow, alerting them that it is probably not a good idea to start with you. Perhaps they have already made a few comments that signal to you they are going to do their best to be the top dog at your expense. Some mild verbal aggression can reduce the potential for threatening or painful situations to evolve.

Since you may be feeling insecure about these situations, it does make more sense to focus your attention on where these insecurities are coming from first. When you do, you reduce the potential and the magnitude of threatening events coming from these types of people. It has the added advantage of making you a stronger person on a more holistic level, a level that does not require verbal aggression.

## RELIEVING THE PRESSURE THAT COMES FROM HOLDING ANGER IN

Holding your anger in usually results from a decision not to confront someone who is threatening you or has the potential to do you harm (flight versus fight). In some situations, they may have already done the damage. You may understand that holding your anger in did nothing to remedy the situation. The more you acquiesce, the more they continue. Running away has caused you to feel weak. Stuffing your feelings raises your anxiety level and may even cause obsessive thoughts about the other person and what they have done to you.

Understanding that your previous methods were unsuccessful, you choose to confront the offender. Your method of confrontation is to verbally attack them. Though you may have given this some thought and put some time between the event and your response, your anger has not subsided, and adrenaline still runs the show. If this were not the case, you may have calmed down enough to examine other alternatives such as attempting to communicate with the other person. However, since the adrenaline rush has not sufficiently diminished, your method of dealing with this person takes on an aggressive posture and verbal weaponry to attack the other person. The reason you go from running away to a planned aggressive attack is that you have not yet become proficient at an assertive confrontation without aggression. That is the middle ground. It is the intermediate step that is missing in your delivery.

In situations where you are moving from flight (running and stuffing your feelings) to fight (standing your ground and confronting), it is important to understand how to efficiently represent your position and, if possible, with a reduction of emotion. You have no control over what the other person will do. You *do* have control over what you do. Your goal is to establish your boundaries and be willing to defend those boundaries.

I discussed boundary-setting and defense in detail in *The Fix Yourself Handbook*. To the point, when a person does something that hurts you or violates your boundaries, it is important to let them know, clearly and succinctly, what they have done and what you will no longer tolerate. It is also important to express this calmly. By doing so, you move from being a person who runs away from what you fear to someone willing to assertively confront someone who has hurt you. This will go a long way in your quest to remove anger from your life.

## OVERT REPRESENTATIONS OF ONE'S INTERNAL THOUGHT PROCESSES

At times, you may have what seems to be a short fuse and react with potent aggression, verbally attacking someone for something they have said or done. Usually, those verbally aggressive episodes are expressed as the result of internal thoughts that are angry and fearful and are designed to even the score.

Before the anger is even expressed, obsessive thoughts that accompany unresolved situations are already at play. This happens when someone has done something that causes you to react with anger, but you do not confront the person about what has occurred. Instead, you are left with unresolved thoughts about what happened, and those thoughts replay in your mind. You may even have internal conversations with the other person in which you tell them off. This can provide some temporary relief since the internal rehearsal symbolically puts the other person in their place.

The problem is that each time the obsessive thoughts occur and you perform this score-evening ritual, you become angrier because the situation is not resolved, so you continue to feel the fear and pain associated with it. Sooner or later, you are going to find yourself, once again, in that anger-provoking situation. It may be with the same person or someone who hurts or similarly offends you. Now, you unleash a verbal barrage designed to quickly sever their emotional jugular and render them defenseless. In some cases, you may get your point across. In other cases, the person rises to the occasion, and the battle begins.

The problem associated with obsessive thinking about unresolved anger is that it becomes a default way of living life. It does not have to be relegated to people who have hurt you. You become an obsessive-aggressive thinker, whose negative energy can propel much of your internal thought processes. The advice here is simple: If you have frequent angry thoughts and a reasonable amount of your internal language is negative or aggressive, it is a tip-off that you need to do something about it. This is where friends and a professional counselor come into the picture. If you cannot resolve it on your own internally, and if confronting another person peacefully isn't working, maybe it is time to talk about it with someone who can help. Staying *in your own head* while attempting to resolve matters that need to be resolved in the external world rarely, if ever, works. Becoming someone who learns how to reduce oppressive internal thinking sets the stage for thoughts and behaviors that bring peace and productivity into your life.

## TO MASK FEAR

For some people, nothing masks fear better than anger. Let's look at fear as the catalyst for the flight response and anger as the enforcer for the fight response. One of the misconceptions about the fight-or-flight response is that when we stay and fight, we are confident about what we are about to do and do not fear our opponent. This is not always the case. People may engage in battle precisely because they fear being hurt, traumatized, or, in extreme cases, even killed. So, staying to fight doesn't always mean you are confident that you can defeat your adversary. Sometimes, you will stay and fight simply because you believe you have no other option.

When you choose to run from the situation, your fear of that situation is readily observable. You see the danger, fear what might happen, and quickly remove yourself from the situation. You have chosen to live to fight (or run) another day. The difference between fighting even though you are afraid and running because you are afraid is simply a matter of staying or leaving. In each case, however, fear can be the motivating factor.

If one has the skills to successfully broker arguments, they do not need to rely on fighting one's way through them. The question is, why fight when you can negotiate? The answer is that fear overrides your intellectual skills, and the decision to counterattack is made abruptly. No one wants to be seen as weak and fearful. In the case of standing your ground and fighting your adversary in the face of fear, the aggression being expressed through verbal assaults creates the appearance of being in control and unafraid. The goal is to move your adversary off their position of strength by creating the appearance that you are strong. The adage that the best defense is a strong offense is running the discourse. So, verbal anger is often used to ward off attacks and perceived attacks before they can develop into a threatening or dangerous experience.

Once again, the key is that in situations where verbal aggression is used to mask underlying fear, more efficient strategies are being abandoned, with a return to a more primal way of interacting. It is important to develop skills to communicate your position, instead of using verbal anger to drive someone back. You might find your confidence in your ability to communicate through a difficult situation rather than verbally beating your way through it. In the next chapter, I discuss fear-based anger and how to rise above it.

## SECURELY SPEAKING

So much of the use of verbal anger is an outgrowth of fear and our difficulty communicating with each other. Verbal aggression is like screaming, "I am afraid and don't know what to do!" to those on the receiving end of this type of anger. Also, almost nothing is ever settled by using verbal attacks. People on the receiving end are inundated with volume, aggression, and threatening body language. The message you are attempting to communicate is often smothered by the anger you are expressing. Learning to communicate what is bothering you more warmly to another person goes a long way in getting your point across to someone you feel needs to understand your message. There is a chapter on warm communication in *The Fix Yourself Handbook*.

 **TIME TO TAKE ACTION**

1. List the types of verbal anger you tend to use. Before you can make changes, you need to know if and how you are using language to control others.

2. Think about why you are using verbal anger. It is easy to blame the other person, but this decision is yours. Be honest here.

3. In any situation where you became verbally aggressive, think about how you may have handled it differently. It is a good idea to talk to others you trust about this.

4. Give some thought to your insecurities and how they might motivate you to use verbal aggression.

5. Pay close attention to your internal language. Do you often think angry thoughts? Are you having internal conversations to sort through difficult situations? If you are, it makes sense to talk it over with someone you trust.

**6.** It is a good idea to keep a journal to help you review each day and how often you either felt angry or experienced angry thoughts. Pay special attention to how often you may have used verbal anger with others.

**7.** It is up to you to control how you think and react. You cannot stop others from creating situations that have an impact on you, but you *can* learn to control what you do about it. If you are having difficulty controlling your emotions, it is a good idea to contact a professional counselor.

 ## Driving It Home

Verbal anger may indicate that you are afraid or have unresolved insecurities. Anyone can get into an argument or, at the very least, raise their voice on occasion. The concern is how often it happens and how intense it becomes. No one likes to be verbally assaulted. Rarely, if ever, do verbal assaults accomplish anything other than heightening emotions in an already difficult situation. Learning to communicate effectively sets the stage for less anger, efficient communicative options, and a much happier way to live.

**YOUR DECLARATION IS**: *I will respect others and myself by learning how to communicate without anger!*

 ## Onward

In this chapter, we began to discuss how anger can be used to mask fears and insecurities. In the next chapter, I will show you how fear can be the underlying motivator for anger. I will also show you some ways to face your fears *before* they turn into angry outbursts.

CHAPTER 4

# Fear-Based Anger: The Mask

*Anger makes you feel strong and in control, but it is nothing more than a mask you created to hide your fears and insecurities.*

**PROCESSES TO EMPLOY:** Brutal Honesty, I Over E, Present/Understand/Fix, Slowing Down Life's Pace, Internal Focus, Fact-Finding, One-Day-at-a-Time Living, Living in the Moment, Settling Past Issues, Life Inventory

ANGER DOES NOT ALWAYS HAVE A STRAIGHTFORWARD presentation. It can also be expressed to hide other emotions, particularly fear. Sometimes, it is easier to be mad than scared. A traditional definition of "fear" is *an unpleasant emotion caused by the belief that someone or something is dangerous, and likely to cause pain or a threat.* If you are experiencing fear in a threatening situation, you may temporarily rise above that fear, and use anger to thwart off your potential oppressor. For many people, using anger to mask fear is a normal way to live.

## THAT CREATIVE THINKING MACHINE

In Chapter 1, I introduced your brain as a sophisticated thinking machine that either controls or is involved in the operation of every system in the body. Your brain is a powerful, sophisticated organ that is cunning enough to provide you with creative options to rescue you from serious threats. It can also provide you with productive options to enhance the quality of your life. When your brain substitutes anger for fear, it rearranges the way you would usually react in a fear-producing situation and turns it into one where you feel more confident.

Regardless of whether you fight or flee, both reactions can be motivated by fear. At times, when the traditional fight-or-flight response engages, anger is the provoking catalyst to turn you into a fighting machine, while fear motivates you to run. But what happens when you become fearful in a threatening situation but choose *not* to run? You have two options:

1. You can remain in the situation as a fearful person.
2. You can stay in this situation but present yourself as someone capable of meeting the challenge head-on.

In the first instance, people stay in a threatening situation despite the potential harm to them. When this occurs, what we most often see is a person who does not have much to say and is willing to take their oppressor's abuse. This often occurs in cases of bullying where the victim is cowering, attempting to please their oppressor, and leaving the situation emotionally humiliated, intellectually torn apart, and at times, hurt physically.

The second option is the one we are interested in. In this storyline, the person is scared and would like to run. Intellectually and emotionally, they are processing their fear. They are aware that they are feeling afraid. They are uncomfortable and know that running is an option. However, they have chosen to stay and fight. Why do this when running is a safer choice? Here are a few reasons:

- They may be protecting someone close to them.
- Their fear may be so emotionally overwhelming that they act without thinking.
- They may have run so often and have been made to feel like a coward. They may feel that staying in the fight, even if there's a potential for physical harm, is the better option.

- They may have decided in conjunction with their counselor or advisor to face their fear.

## MASKED UP

There are many ways people substitute one emotion or life condition for another. In *The Fix Your Depression Handbook*, I discuss when a person can be depressed and, at times, need to be in the presence of other people. They may not want anyone else to know that they are depressed, so they will put on a happy mask to hide their depression. Another example is the person who struggles with a pedestrian-like intellect and would like others to believe they are intelligent. So, they consistently provide what they believe is intellectual information on any variety of subjects to mask their run-of-the-mill intellectual capacity.

Few people are comfortable with having others believe they are fearful people. We all like to be perceived as capable. So, in situations where we might respond by either running away or surrendering to an oppressor, another option might be to show strength, even though it is nothing more than an emotional coverup. Here is an example:

> Stella is an eighteen-year-old senior in high school. She is an honor student and a member of the school's track team, where she excels in the 100-yard dash. Two of the other girls on the team do not have Stella's athletic prowess. They typically finish in the bottom third in their events, and in school, they are average students. Stella comes from a supportive family, and the rule has always been to take the high road and walk away from a fight. Stella believes this is the correct way to behave and has always followed through with this advice.
>
> The two girls have consistently teased her and made degrading comments both in school and on the track field. Feeling that they are only comments and firmly believing that if she ignores them, they will stop, Stella has always simply walked away from them. Other students have seen her do this. A few

of Stella's close friends understand what is happening and are supportive. Others, however, see Stella as weak and afraid. Last week, one of the girls pushed her she while was training for an event, causing some minor scrapes on Stella's knees.

Both girls are competing in events that require more strength, and both are stronger than Stella. Stella knows that if she stands and defends herself, she will probably get hurt. Now Stella has a decision to make. She can't simply ignore the physical abuse as she did with their verbal onslaughts. Stella is either going to run and feel like a coward, or she is going to stand her ground and risk injury. Stella decides to fight fire with fire.

Today one of the girls, once again, pushed Stella as she was training. Stella fell but then rose, screaming at the girl, and started throwing punches. Though Stella was afraid, she did not show her fear. All anyone saw was an angry outburst. No one expected this from their good-mannered and timid teammate. The girl who pushed Stella did engage in battle with her, though no one got hurt. In the end, by using anger to mask her fear, Stella received respect from the other girls, and they stopped abusing her.

## FROM MASK TO STRATEGY

Stella's story is an example of anger masking fear in a particular situation. However, what happens when people use the anger mask as a default way of behaving with others? Again, the human mind is a marvelous thinking machine. In the example, not only did Stella create a temporary persona that allowed her to defend herself, but her mind understood that the strategy had worked. Now, Stella understands that this plan of action is available to her, and she can call upon it when she needs it. The human mind doesn't abandon useful strategies; it calls upon or incorporates successful strategies to be used in future situations. Here is a second example to illustrate this:

Harold is a sixteen-year-old sophomore in high school. He comes from a blended family and lives with his mother and his stepfather. His mother is supportive and tries to do her best to take care of her son. Harold's stepfather is a tough individual with a drinking problem. Harold's mother and his stepfather have been together for five years. Harold's stepfather doesn't think much of him, and Harold must deal with his verbal assaults daily. At times, when the man drinks, Harold has been on the receiving end of physical abuse.

When Harold was younger, he took the abuse and hid from his stepfather as often as he could. Now, at sixteen years old, he has begun to physically mature and is a member of the high school wrestling team. Harold lifts weights and trains several times per week with his friends who are also on the team. Earlier in the year, on an evening when his stepfather was drinking and being verbally abusive to his mother, Harold stepped in and became physical, pushing his stepfather, who fell backward. Though he was fearful of what might happen to him or his mother, his anger got the best of him, and from that day forward, his stepfather avoided him.

Living in a home where anger and abuse were daily occurrences, Harold took a chance and rose above his fear, as he confronted his oppressor. Harold also understood that he could control these situations since his stepfather was now afraid of him. Harold learned two things: First, he learned that he could fend off an oppressor by using anger when he was afraid. Second, and more important, he understood that he could control other people with his anger.

Harold used to be a mild-mannered student, but recently he is showing more anger, and people are beginning to avoid him. Using anger did not stop Harold from being afraid, but it did show him that if he uses an angry mask more often, he can control other people and be more in control of his world. Now, anger has evolved from a response to a threatening situation to one that is used to control situations to make sure the threat never happens in the first place.

What started as a survival strategy to help protect Harold from a potential or imminent threat evolved into a way of life. We all use masks to move through our environment. They can protect us from people who could hurt us, but they also help us keep others from acquiring information about us that we would prefer to stay private. In the example with Stella, she didn't want anyone to know she was scared so anger masked the fear she was experiencing. Her angry outburst told her abusers that, in no uncertain terms, their behavior would not be tolerated. Harold, on the other hand, began by using anger to mask his fear, but he learned that he could use it to maintain control in his environment and to establish a way of life that kept abuse away from him before it had a chance to begin.

As you will see, the goal is to become a person who does not have to use anger. In Stella's case, the first order of business was to attempt to reason with the two girls. She needed to do this from a position of confidence. You never *ask* someone to stop abusing you; you make it clear to them that the behavior will not be tolerated. Stella's movement to anger was a last resort and served the purpose in that instance, but it was not something she planned to use for the rest of her life.

Harold saw the advantage of continuing to use his angry mask. Sometimes this does keep potential abusers at bay. Other times, however, would-be abusers may try to call the other person's bluff. An angry mask used as a permanent shield will only last until someone stronger challenges it. At the very least, Harold has redefined his life by using anger to address situations that could be solved by using other methods. Now, people may perceive that he is an angry person, which may affect his relationships.

Learning how to efficiently reduce anger has more to do with settling internal issues than it does with wearing external masks. This doesn't mean that situational masks can't serve a purpose. The danger is in living behind them and not honestly addressing what happens in your life. Sooner or later, people see behind the mask. It is much easier to learn to become stronger on the inside than it is to attempt to mask feelings like fear with strength. The rule of thumb is to always work from the inside, as you will see as we continue in Part Two.

**TIME TO TAKE ACTION**

1. List all the scenarios in your life that cause you to become fearful or uncomfortable.

2. Try to determine where the fear is coming from in each of those situations.

3. Now, list all the situations you wanted to run from but used anger to mask the fear you were experiencing.

4. For each of the situations in which you used anger, write down exactly what you did when you used your angry mask.

5. Examine each of the times you used anger to see if there might have been other ways to deal with it.

6. Fear that develops into anger may have roots in unresolved past issues. If you continue to use anger to mask fear, it is important to address past issues. If you are having trouble doing this on your own, enlist the help of a professional counselor.

 **DRIVING IT HOME**

Fear and anger seem to be at opposite ends of the spectrum. However, one can lead to the other, and at times, they can occur simultaneously. When you use an angry mask to hide your fear, you are experiencing fear and anger at the same time. Your anger may mask the fear and help you through a difficult situation, but it does not get to the heart of the matter. It does not help you face your fear. The important takeaway from this chapter is that even if the anger does what you want it to do in any situation where fear is involved, it is only a mask, and sooner or later, you will have to face the person behind the mask.

**YOUR DECLARATION IS:** *I will put down my angry mask and learn to face my world honestly!*

 **ONWARD**

Life doesn't always go as planned, and sometimes people and events can cause you to feel frustrated. Frustration can set the table for anger and angry outbursts. In the next chapter, I examine frustration-based anger, how it develops, and what you can do about it.

CHAPTER 5

# Frustration-Based Anger: The End of the Rope

*Frustration can come from outside sources, or it can live deep inside you. Frustration is a breeding ground for an angry life.*

**PROCESSES TO EMPLOY:** Brutal Honesty, I Over E, Present/Understand/Fix, Slowing Down Life's Pace, Internal Focus, Fact-Finding, Living in the Moment, Settling Past Issues, Life Inventory

ANYONE CAN BECOME FRUSTRATED. Sometimes, frustration is a result of our unmet expectations or repeated failures. Other times, it has to do with other people and situations that repeatedly cause problems for us, as we perceive them. Sometimes, it is merely a representation of our dissatisfaction with our lives. Let's define "frustration" as *the feeling of being upset or annoyed, especially because of the inability to stop, change, or achieve something.* Something happens or does not happen, and if this repeatedly occurs, various degrees of frustration arise, depending on the duration and intensity of the event.

While frustration is often thought of as a common emotion that people feel when things do not go the way they want them to go, this is not the whole story. The rise in emotion that accompanies frustration is the result of anger. Moreover, ongoing bouts of irritability (a feeling of agitation) often result in anger-fueled frustration. Many things can cause us to be irritable—from stress and anxiety to depression and physical pain. Other culprits include lack of sleep, relationship and financial issues, chronic pain, repeated failure, and poor self-image. Regardless of the terminology, being irritable often results in getting easily frustrated or upset, and anger is the result.

## COMMON CAUSES OF FRUSTRATION

There are many causes of frustration. Some come from repeated difficult people and events, while others may come from our self-image and the perceptions that arise as a result.

- **AN UNEXPECTED TURN OF EVENTS**: Many people have difficulty with change and quick transitions. Irritability can easily arise when something happens that demands a change from what was expected. When this occurs, especially repeatedly, frustration can quickly set in. These are the more prominent causes:

- **FINANCIAL PROBLEMS**: Life can be difficult if you are living paycheck to paycheck and struggling to pay your bills. If you cannot seem to make ends meet, and there is no light at the end of the financial tunnel, worry and frustration can set in.

- **UNRESOLVED CONFLICTS**: One of the most potent instigators of frustration is pressure from others and problematic, unresolved situations in your life. This creates an undercurrent of frustration, which is a huge catalyst for anger. (I will be discussing more about the undercurrents of frustration shortly.)

- **FAILING OR UNHEALTHY RELATIONSHIPS**: Relationship issues, especially those that are not resolved, are a breeding ground for anxiety, depression, and agitation. Attempts to repair the relationship without success can produce frustration along with the angry thoughts and behaviors that follow.

- **UNHEALTHY WORK ENVIRONMENTS**: Difficulties with supervisors and other employees can produce work environments that lead to worry, agitation, and frustration. Eventually, anger can develop, exacerbating employment concerns.

- **ACCELERATED PACE OF LIFE**: Trying to keep up with an unreasonable daily schedule leads to an accelerated life pace, which produces agitation and anger. Going too fast causes physical, emotional, and intellectual pressure. It might feel like you never get things right and as though you never measure up to your standards or those of others.

- **UNFULFILLED SEXUAL DESIRES:** Sexual tension is an extremely strong motivator for frustration. Performance issues, emotional intimacy problems, rejection, and personal distance in relationships can lead to feelings of inadequacy and produce severe self-esteem issues. When this is an ongoing problem, frustration can develop, and anger often follows.

- **QUICK TEMPER:** For some people, angry outbursts seem to be a way of life. They have short internal fuses, and angry outbursts usually follow the overwhelming internal frustration.

- **ANXIETY, DEPRESSION, AND/OR POST-TRAUMATIC STRESS DISORDER (PTSD):** Dealing with mental health issues can easily set the stage for frustration. Mental health disorders such as depression, anxiety, and PTSD, as I discuss in both *The Fix Your Anxiety Handbook* and *The Fix Your Depression Handbook*, can cause frustration since the individual never seems to find a way out of them. Also, someone living with these conditions we'll have a more difficult time working through situations. Frustration is often the end result

## COMMON SIGNS OF FRUSTRATION

Frustration can manifest in many ways. People who are frustrated usually become irritable and stressed, some more quickly than others. While frustration can be a seemingly justified reaction to an unpleasant situation, other times, it can be an overreaction to something inconsequential. Common signs of frustration include:

- **LOSING YOUR TEMPER:** The most obvious sign of frustration, this is when you scream, throw things, have tantrums, and verbally (sometimes physically) release your anger on another person.

- **INCESSANT BODY MOVEMENTS**: As frustration moves from your brain and throughout your nervous system, you will experience irritable leg movements, tapping your fingers, fidgeting, and having difficulty staying in one place.

- **CHANGES IN HEART RATE AND BREATHING**: Anger is always accompanied by physical acceleration. When this happens, your heart rate will increase, you will breath faster, and as a result, take in more carbon dioxide which reduced the amount of oxygen available to your cells. You will take deeper breaths and, at times, have difficulty catching your breath.

- **GIVING UP AND LEAVING**: If you believe you have exhausted all the possible ways to fix the frustrating situation without success, you may feel like you are at the end of your rope—that is, you lack the patience and energy to keep trying. At this point, throwing your hands up and leaving the situation relieves at least some of the tension.

- **FEELING SAD OR ANXIOUS**: Quite often, there is no solution in a frustrating situation; feeling anxious as a result can be expected. Without a solution to your dilemma, a period of sadness sets in. Dealing with frustration can be physically and mentally exhausting.

- **REDUCTION IN SELF-ESTEEM AND SELF-CONFIDENCE**: People who are frustrated often verbalize negative feelings and think that no matter what they do, nothing works out for them. This can have a profound effect on one's self-esteem and self-confidence.

- **TROUBLE SLEEPING**: Since frustration leads to anxiety, you might experience some difficulty sleeping. It may be difficult to fall asleep as your mind continues to dwell on frustrating situations, or you may wake up during the night from time to time and have difficulty falling back to sleep.

- **TURNING TO ALCOHOL AND OTHER DRUGS**: Substance abuse and anger go hand in hand. The physical, intellectual, and emotional stress frustration causes may motivate you to do something to "turn off" your mind, calm your emotions, and soothe your body. Alcohol and other drugs are often the first choices.

- **BODILY ABUSE, STARVING ONESELF, OR IRREGULAR EATING HABITS**: In more extreme cases of frustration, those that are intense and of long duration, some people elect to soothe themselves by performing rituals like cutting and other forms of physical abuse. Also, since the accelerated life pace can make it more difficult to eat regularly, periods of self-starvation may occur. I discuss self-abusive anger in Chapter 15.

## AN UNDERCURRENT OF FRUSTRATION

As mentioned, sometimes what you are reacting to with frustration-based anger is not the primary concern at that moment. Frustrating people and situations without resolution that repeatedly affect you can create an undercurrent of frustration. This means you are *always* frustrated, although you may not routinely focus on those frustrating concerns. For example, you have financial concerns that have affected your relationship with your partner; while you are engaged in a home repair that is not going well, you take your anger out on the object you are trying to repair. The object obviously had no power to create the response, but the undercurrent of frustration, which is always there, kept you primed and ready to react.

## 7 KEYS TO HELP YOU REDUCE YOUR FRUSTRATION-BASED ANGER

Becoming frustrated can quickly lead to angry outbursts. The following are seven strategies you can use to help reduce your frustration, and subsequently, the anger that can follow.

1. Try to put closure on recurring issues in your life such as difficulty with friends and family.

2. Get a handle on any financial issues. If you need help, consider enlisting the aid of a financial advisor.

3. Attempt to reconcile any relationship differences with those close to you. If you are unable to do this together, consider going for professional couples/relationship counseling.

4. Address any unpleasant issues at work. For example, if you have an issue with a coworker or supervisor and you cannot resolve this by speaking with the other person, consider bringing the matter to your human resources department. If you cannot resolve the ongoing frustrating work issue, you might want to consider seeking alternate employment.

5. Slow down the pace of your life. It is hard to find solutions to problems when you are moving too fast and simply do not have enough time to think about what to do.

6. Try to resolve past events that tend to move forward with you. Traumas, abuse, and other sources of past pain are breeding grounds for frustration and anger. You may need help with this from outside sources like friends, family, or professionals.

7. If nothing you have tried works to relieve your frustration, consider seeking the help of a professional counselor. If you do not fully understand why you are frustrated, it makes sense to let someone help.

## MOVING IN THE RIGHT DIRECTION

Anyone can get frustrated. Sometimes a triggering event causes feelings of overwhelm, thereby resulting in a frustrated, angry response. Other times, unresolved issues with people and recurring situations create an undercurrent of frustration. That said, frustration may simply be a way of thinking and behaving that your brain has become accustomed to. Regardless, being perpetually frustrated and angry does not have to be the way you live your life. All too often, we feel as though we are backed into a corner with no way out. There is always a way out, and it does not have to be something that causes you additional pain.

Putting closure on difficult situations can go a long way toward helping you remove any frustration permeating your life. Those undercurrents are either from something in the past or something current in your life that is not being resolved. Frustration usually means you have tried everything you can to fix something but continue to fail. This does not mean there is no solution; it simply means you haven't found it. Frustration is one of those emotional responses that causes a reduction in clarity of thought, causing negative thinking and making problems seem unsolvable. If you find yourself unable to put closure on situations and reduce the frustration in your life, it is a good time to consider getting help. There is no shame in asking for help, and it may be the first step you take in creating a life with far less frustration and much more happiness.

##  TIME TO TAKE ACTION

1. List the frustrating circumstances in your life. Refer to the causes of frustration earlier in the chapter. Talk about the items on your list with someone you trust. This can help you address them more efficiently with people who could help you.

2. Take a good look at unresolved past issues such as abuse and other traumas. Try to determine if they are still causing pain in your life today.

3. Refer to the signs of frustration earlier in the chapter. If you are experiencing any of these signs, make note of them. These are also items that can be discussed in counseling situations.

4. Refer to the "7 Keys to Help Reduce Your Frustration-Based Anger" to help you address your frustration. Share this information with someone you trust if you are having difficulty applying the keys.

5. If you cannot resolve frustrating circumstances in your life despite your efforts, or if past issues continue to cause you frustration and anger, it is a good idea to contact a professional counselor. It is much better to get help to address these issues than to continue to be frustrated and angry about them.

 **Driving It Home**

Frustration can be a very strong catalyst for angry thinking and behaviors. Consistently becoming frustrated lays the groundwork for a negative lifestyle, which seems to have no end. Becoming aware of the past and present conditions in your life that can cause you to become annoyed, overwhelmed, and eventually frustrated is the first step in addressing this anger-causing emotional response. If you cannot find solutions to the causes of your frustration, it makes sense to ask for help. Frustration often comes from unresolved issues, but there is always a way to put closure on them. Being less frustrated opens the door to a life with much less anger and far more peace.

**YOUR DECLARATION IS**: *I will identify the sources of my frustration and will find solutions to them!*

 **Onward**

There are many observable and definable causes of anger. Pain, especially chronic pain, can lurk in the background and reduce your body's ability to cope with challenging life circumstances. In the next chapter, I discuss pain-based anger, how it develops, and what you can do about it.

CHAPTER 6

# Pain-Based Anger: Internal Attacks

*Pain is real, and so is the anger it creates. Positive energy is always one's best ally.*

**PROCESSES TO EMPLOY:** Brutal Honesty, I Over E, Present/Understand/Fix, Slowing Down Life's Pace, Internal Focus, Fact-Finding, Living in the Moment, Settling Past Issues

MOST PEOPLE EXPERIENCE PAIN AT SOME POINT in their lives and to varying degrees. Sometimes the pain comes from injury, sometimes it is a function of age, and other times it may be the result of a disease or chronic condition. Regardless of its etiology, most of us do not like to feel pain, and when it continues without relief, it can be an efficient instigator of anger.

As you will see, many personal and environmental conditions can cause you to feel angry. Think about a day when you were in a reasonable amount of pain. Maybe you had a toothache, you threw out your back, or you were recovering from minor surgery. You may have been more reactive, less tolerant of others and challenging situations, and lost your temper more quickly than usual. Your angry response in those instances seems to be your way of saying, "I am in pain, and I am angry."

Aside from the physical discomfort that accompanies pain, you may feel limited in terms of what you can do. Your whole nervous system feels like it is firing at once, and you simply do not feel good.

For an already angry person, pain can bring anger to an entirely new level. People who routinely struggle with anger now have a bona-fide reason to express their dissatisfaction with the current conditions in their lives and with anything and everyone around them. For some, pain seems to give them a license to express their anger.

For people who are not routinely angry, pain can introduce a less-than-tolerant way to think and feel. You might wake up in the morning and your gums are swollen. Your molar is killing you. Now, you find yourself a few minutes late for work, and one of the children can't find their shoes. On a typical day, this may cause you to become a bit reactive, but today you are yelling and having difficulty focusing, and now your tooth is making your life miserable.

## ABUSE FROM THE INSIDE

In *The Fix Your Anxiety Handbook*, I discuss how anxiety can become a condition that feels like you are being abused. I use the term "anxiety demon" and how, after a while, the abuse seems to be coming from inside you. Pain can have the same effect on you. It can feel like a form of internal abuse. Your body is inflicting pain on you, and at least for a while, you can't stop it. For some, chronic pain never leaves, and you may feel like you are being beaten up every day. Forget fight or flight, you can't run away from your pain. Regardless of what you do, you are still in pain.

Pain and anger can have a circular and complementary relationship. First, something begins to hurt. It can have a rapid onset, or it can develop gradually. When it gets to the point that it becomes uncomfortable, you can become a bit more reactive. Things you typically do not have a problem with now seem to be causing more problems than usual. As the pain progresses, you become more uncomfortable, and now your reaction is one of anger. What you may not realize is that as you become angrier, your body becomes more sensitized. Anger always causes more physical and emotional sensitivity. Now, the anger is beginning to feed the pain.

Anger has its way of making everything in your life seem that much worse. You may note if you have ever had surgery or something as simple as having a tooth extracted, the doctor will tell you to go home and relax. They may prescribe painkillers, which have two functions: they reduce the sensitivity in your brain's pain center, and they also have sedative properties that help you relax, even if just a little. The goal is to help you reduce the pain, and the process is to relax, slow down, and stop reacting. Slowing down your body reduces the sensitivity, and that helps you reduce the pain.

## PAIN DOESN'T CARE

Most of us want no part of pain, and we will do anything in our power to avoid it. Of course, pain doesn't know that, and it seems to have a life of its own. It invades your body, plays with your emotions, and robs you of sound intellectual processing. In Jekyll-and-Hyde fashion, you become reduced to an angry, intolerant, and at times, abusive individual. You may throw things. Nothing suits you; you might lash out at other people and be completely dissatisfied with just about everything in your life. Humility and gratitude are on hiatus. You are in pain, and you are angry. That's all!

Everyone has a certain level of pain tolerance. For some, on a scale of one to ten, they may top out at a two or three. Others have a higher threshold, and their threshold may be a seven or an eight. Your pain threshold is where anger begins to make its appearance. For all of us, arriving at our personal threshold is where all the changes begin. This is where we can be introduced to Mr. Hyde. Pain has now reached the point where we are very uncomfortable, and it is beginning to affect our thinking and our emotions.

For some people, pain tolerance is a predetermined setting. These people want no part of pain and will tell themselves that. They may arrive at their threshold before they are physically unable to deal with the duress. They tell themselves, in advance, that they are going to be miserable, and it does not take long before they are. It is always a good idea to understand your pain threshold and not set it in advance. When you establish an accurate pain threshold, you gain just a little more control over the anger, which can result from being so uncomfortable.

## THE FAST, THE FURIOUS, AND THE HERE TO STAY

When it comes to pain-based anger, it is important to understand the distinction between chronic pain and pain with a quick and potent onset. Chronic pain, which can result from conditions like back injuries, recurring migraine headaches, arthritis, and immune system disorders, becomes part of everything you do, every day. Meanwhile, pain with a quick onset is usually the result of injuries, surgery, or other discomforts like pulling a muscle. Even though some of the causes of rapid onset pain may make return visits, they are not part of daily life.

When one experiences rapid-onset pain that invokes anger, two things can happen:

1. You react quickly, possibly throwing something, cursing, or yelling at someone.
2. You can immediately blame someone or something even though they had little or no influence over the occurrence.

Chronic pain that instigates anger follows the same path in your body as anxiety. It begins in your body, works its way quickly to your emotions, and then overrides your intellectual reasoning faculties. When this happens, you lose focus. Your pain is overriding any other sensation in your body. This is perfectly normal since your body, having experienced an injury, is sending as much energy as possible to that location to help you recover from the pain. Unfortunately, when this happens, your emotions and your brain's ability to remain rational are compromised. The only thing you know is that you are in pain, and anyone else's feelings or inanimate objects nearby no longer deserve (as you perceive it) the respect you would normally give them. Having control over your emotional and intellectual functioning is simply not that important to your body when you are in pain.

For the most part, others will understand why you reacted the way you did and you will not have done any permanent damage to your relationships. (The object you hurled across the room that smashed to pieces against the wall is an entirely different story.) When you experience rapid-onset pain and react with anger in front of others, it is a good idea to later explain why you reacted that way and apologize for your quick, out-of-control behavior.

Chronic pain is an entirely different set of circumstances. People who experience chronic pain are in pain most of the time. At times, the level of pain fluctuates, but your body is still trying to address what is happening to you. The pain center is always activated, you are always uncomfortable, and most of your energy is being directed to the painful area. You may be dealing with that for the better part of the day. For some, sleep becomes a problem since the pain does not shut off just because the day has come to an end.

Being in chronic pain is exhausting; it is likely hard to focus on what you are doing or finish what you started, a) you are very uncomfortable, and b) your body simply cannot stay in the same place for a significant amount of time. Emotionally, you have little room or tolerance for anything that elevates your nervous system. So, loud noises, confusion and conflict, other people getting angry, and sometimes just the general commotion of the day can make a bad situation that much worse. Intellectually, your reasoning faculties are *always* being challenged. It is hard to listen to anyone long enough, let alone try to discern what they are saying, organize the facts, and come up with any type of plan to address those facts. Efficient communication always seems to be operating at a minimum.

## CUT ME A BREAK

Some people understand the correlation between pain and anger, and do their best to rise above it. When someone has rapid-onset pain, they can offset any angry behavior with an explanation and an apology. Some of those people, however, operate with an undercurrent of frustration, as I discussed in Chapter 5. In these cases, the anger can persist longer than the pain since the person is already dealing with an angry disposition. While someone who is not routinely angry can apologize quickly and put the matter to rest, for those who operate with anger more often, the aftereffects of the painful episode may persist long after the event, and they may apologize simply to relieve themselves of the responsibility for their actions.

Once again, there are two ways to approach anger related to chronic pain. Though you are in pain and it does affect the way you think, feel, and behave, you can either use it as an excuse and continue to behave angrily, or you can ask for help and do your best to avoid angry outbursts. This might seem like a tall order, and for some people it is. Chronic pain, it is probably not going anywhere. This is where you choose to do as much as you can on any given day, let people help you, and seek the help of a professional counselor, if necessary.

## IT'S REAL, AND IT HURTS, BUT—

No one can tell you that your pain is not real. It is not their body, and they don't feel what you feel. It hurts, and when it does, you can become angry. Those are facts. We have all experienced pain at one level or another, and as long as we continue living, there will be more. That is also a fact. When you are in pain, you may react emotionally and with anger. That anger may have a short shelf life, or it could be an ongoing part of your journey through life. My goal here is not to tell you that you should not be angry when pain invades your life. The key is to learn how to more efficiently respond to the pain so that it doesn't create more problems for you.

In the cases of rapid-onset pain, the best advice is not to blame someone on the spot, throw things, and get completely out of control. The pain hits, sometimes hard, and you will react. Try to direct what you are feeling to the pain. Your brain is designed to help you deal with the pain; attempting to make someone else the focus of your pain is not something your brain is designed to do. So, focus on the pain, and if possible, find a way to deal with it.

In most cases, those who witnessed you getting hurt have not caused your pain. Attacking them with your anger is not going to make you feel any better. Let your brain and its pain center take care of business for you. Take a deep breath and focus on the part of your body that hurts. Pain feels like negative energy, and it is. Positive energy offsets those negative charges, so give your brain as much positive stimulation as you can. The best way to do this is to let other people know that you have pain and let them help you in any way they can. Also, try not to react quickly. This will instigate that circular response between pain and emotional reactions. In the case of rapid-onset pain, avoiding the circular response gives your brain more positive energy to work with. Just try to focus that anger where it belongs (on what is hurting you), and try not to attack others, as doing so will just create more negative energy.

In the case of chronic pain, you are in pain most of the time, and it can be hard to think positively when periods of relief are either brief or nonexistent. On the other hand, with chronic pain, you are not feeling the rapid infusion of pain. This does give your brain enough time to try to deal with the pain in a more productive fashion. You are still in pain, but your brain can determine how to address it. This, of course, correlates with how intense the pain is every day. The advice is the same: try to keep as calm as you can, and ask others for help. It may also make sense to include a pain-management professional to help you more efficiently address your discomfort.

Always try to focus on what you can do about your chronic pain. As mentioned earlier, becoming angry with others because you are in pain only makes your situation more painful. Understandably, you are in significant pain much of the time, and those around you should consider that. However, it is also important not to use chronic pain as an excuse for expressing anger and aggression to others who may have nothing to do with the reason you are in pain. It is not only about being considerate to them but also about mitigating as much of the pain as you can by dealing directly with your anger.

A simple piece of advice is to do as much as you can to make your body as healthy as it can be, particularly in cases of chronic pain. Improper diets, excessive weight, stimulants, substance abuse, and anything that compromises the health of your body will only make your pain worse. Again, focus on what you can do to help yourself, and let other people help you if they can. Pain will always be part of the human condition, but ensure that you are doing everything you can to give yourself the best opportunity to reduce its impact on your life.

## ⏱ Time to Take Action

1. In the case of rapid-onset pain, keep your focus on the pain and away from angry outbursts toward others.

2. Never make excuses for angry outbursts following painful experiences. Acknowledge what you have done, and apologize quickly, if necessary.

3. Chronic pain can cause you to feel angry often. It puts limitations on what you can do, and those limitations can contribute to angry feelings. Do what you are capable of doing, and keep your body as healthy as you can.

4. It is a good idea to discuss what happens following pain-related angry outbursts (whether due to rapid or chronic pain) to help others understand what you are feeling in those situations. Sharing the facts can be helpful to you while making it easier for them to help you.

5. If you are unwilling to apologize after a rapid-onset painful experience, you may have some unaddressed undercurrents of anger. If you cannot stop the angry outburst and refuse to examine the situation, something else may be going on. Talking it over with someone you trust or a professional counselor makes sense.

6. If you are dealing with chronic pain, pain management can help, but it also makes sense to talk about your feelings and experiences surrounding the pain. Think about including a professional counselor in your pain-management plan.

 **DRIVING IT HOME**

We all experience pain and will continue to experience pain, at least from time to time. Those are facts. Like any other situation, there is what happens, and there is what we choose to do with it. So often, pain sets the table for anger. Try to focus on what you need to do to either alleviate the pain or keep it from getting worse. If others are willing to help you, let them. Reacting to pain with anger does not eliminate the pain. The neurological acceleration that occurs as a result of your angry explosion will only make matters worse. If you react, apologize quickly. If you have chronic pain, create a plan to help you deal with it daily. It is all about keeping your energy as positive as you can. That may be difficult when you are in pain, but even small movements forward can reduce the anger caused by pain and minimize any collateral damage.

**YOUR DECLARATION IS:** *I focus my attention on minimizing my pain, not on expressing my anger!*

 **ONWARD**

Difficult people and challenging situations will always enter our lives. Sometimes, the impact they have on our lives will be insignificant. Other times, however, they may cause angry reactions that only exacerbate a difficult situation. In the next chapter, I discuss reactive anger, how it develops, and what you can do about it.

CHAPTER 7

# Reactive Anger: At the Breaking Point

*Difficult people and situations will never stop invading your life. Stop overreacting to them and learn how to respond productively.*

**PROCESSES TO EMPLOY:** Brutal Honesty, I Over E, Present/Understand/Fix, Slowing Down Life's Pace, Internal Focus, Fact-Finding, Living in the Moment, Settling Past Issues, Life Inventory

**IN THE ORDINARY COURSE OF LIFE,** we all encounter people and situations that trigger quick reactions because we perceive the behavior or situation to be unfair or inconsiderate and/or because it occurs repeatedly. When this happens, we may quickly react to the wrongdoing by becoming angry. Consider this example: You are driving down the road and come to a stop sign. You stop, look both ways and when the coast is clear, you begin to move into the intersection. Suddenly, without warning, a car runs the opposing stop sign. You catch sight of it out of the corner of your eye, immediately step on the brake, and avoid the accident. Then you scream and gesture, letting the traffic rule-breaker know exactly how you feel about their dangerous behavior.

Reactive aggression (also known as impulsive aggression) is often defined as aggressive behavior in response to a perceived threat or provocation. Someone does something, and you quickly and impulsively overreact to what you perceive is being done to you. The other person may or may not have intended to harm you or get you angry, but your reactions are quick and severe. It happens, and there is almost no time between the occurrence and your reaction to it. Your brain simply does not have the time to interpret any information, and in a flash, you become angry and fire back.

For our purposes, let's define "reactive anger" as *a quick and impulsive angry response to a person or event without intellectual interpretation or intervention.* The quick response is what sets this type of anger in motion. In previous chapters, I discussed how beneficial it is to give yourself some time to think before you react with anger. In reactive anger, the defining measure is the absence of intellectual mediation. Your brain has no time to interpret the information relevant to the episode and, subsequently, no time to consider any plausible options. Some examples of reactive anger are:

1. Getting angry when things don't go the way you think they should go or the way you planned.

2. Quickly responding negatively or rudely when you are perceiving someone else as being rude to you.

3. Reacting quickly to your assumption that a worst-case scenario will play out.

4. Saying hurtful things to someone in the moment out of anger or frustration.

5. Jumping to conclusions before someone finishes what they are saying.

In each example, it is important to note two qualifying characteristics that help define reactive anger:

A) The reactions are quick and without much thought about what has happened.

B) The reactions are irrational—that is, they are overblown and emotional.

## GETTING EVEN

When someone does something that puts you at a disadvantage, your mind may quickly go into retribution mode. Since the reaction to the episode is happening quickly, and there is no time to think about what to do, emotions take over and you prepare to even the score (that's the fight part of the fight-or-flight response). If the perpetrator remains nearby, you can verbally attack them and let them know how and why their actions were out of line, ridiculous, or dangerous and how angry they made you feel. If they have put distance between you, your only recourse may be to shout obscenities and make rude gestures, accompanied by the usual less-than-complimentary body language.

It is important to keep in mind that this type of anger is a quick reaction. The important features are *quick* and *reactive*. Reactive anger rarely, if ever, has an intellectual component associated with its release. The human brain is designed to process information in seconds. That is essential to our survival, and it helps us process information quickly enough to not only decide on a course of action but also to clear intellectual space for what we will be presented with next. Neurologically then, things can happen fast.

As our brains become more proficient in processing information on an intellectual basis, they can perform this task with increasing speed and efficiency. This is essential to our continued survival and increases the likelihood that the information we are processing is accurate and that our response to it is rational and actionable. However, what happens in a situation when this dynamic power machine, robbed of its ability to process information efficiently, feels the need to quickly react to something it perceives as threatening or disrespectful? It may react to something that is incorrectly perceived. This is where additional problems can begin.

## "RESPOND DON'T REACT" COMPROMISED

When we are growing up, in one way or another, parents, teachers, and other adults reinforce the notion that we should respond rather than react to any given situation. The unstated goal of this advice was to help us understand that there is, in fact, processing time necessary to collect information that pertains to the present situation, understand it, arrange it into an intelligent presentation, formulate a plan, and act on that plan intelligently. This is why intelligent processing produces slower reaction times; it doesn't take forever, but it does require sufficient time.

Since reactive anger is an instantaneous response, it violates every part of the "respond don't react" paradigm. Reactive anger goes fast. There is little, if any, review of the facts, and no time to understand what to do with the information the facts produce. You do not have any time to think, organize, plan, and respond. You are emotional, and you leapfrog the data collection and interpretation part of the formula. You go right to the conclusion. You react. Needless to say, a reaction that follows a threatening or disrespectful event, followed by little to no intellectual interpretation, and without an efficient plan of action, has a high probability of being emotional and irrational. It often does absolutely nothing to address the situation and may even generate an angry reciprocal response from the object of your anger.

In Chapter 5, I introduced the idea of undercurrents. These underswells of unresolved trauma, abuse, disrespect, and even situations in your life that continue to create feelings of inadequacy, victimization, and disrespect can make you feel as though anger never really leaves you. Reactive anger can take you from zero to a hundred in a fraction of a second. As an angry engine continues to idle, those undercurrents can prime you to react in situations that unconsciously remind you of past pain and unresolved issues, or because they keep you thinking and behaving as an angry person.

## SITUATIONAL OR CONSTANT

Since no two people are the same, no two people possess the same motivating factors that instigate reactive anger in the same way. Everyone has their own personal timeline, and on that timeline, our experiences, our interpretations of those experiences, and our feelings about them can be remarkably different from someone else's. In addition, we all have individualized genetic wiring. This combination invariably produces responses and reactions to situations and other people that are completely unique.

Some people can place painful and traumatic events of the past in a rational perspective. When they find themselves in threatening or compromising situations, their reaction time is a bit longer, and they have just a little more opportunity to interpret information, organize that information, choose what to do, and put that simple plan into action. Typically, in this situation, an angry reaction to a person follows a bit more thought and is often expressed with less intensity. Only under periods of extreme duress might they react with a bit more intensity. These are *situational* reactors.

*Constant* reactors, on the other hand, tend to hold on more tightly to pain and victimization from past issues. They are more likely to be classified as angry people or, at the very least, as people who react quickly in their daily life situations. Others may watch what they say around them with the understanding that they may react quickly with a verbal assault. Constant reactors have a history of reactive anger and may even boast about giving someone "a piece of their mind" and "setting them straight."

It doesn't matter if someone purposefully did something to them or intended no malice whatsoever. Angry reactors, especially constant reactors, may display the following angry reactions when they feel provoked:

➤ They may shout obscenities.

➤ They may make obscene gestures.

➤ They may hurl insults to the point of causing victimization.

➤ They may damage property.

➤ They may cause physical pain or injury.

Though this type of anger is called reactive anger, the angry reactor is often the person who sets the angry situation in motion.

They firmly believe that others are doing or have done something *to them* so they react, but often, they are already primed to react to any possible situation. They are looking for a reason to become angry, and they are also looking for objects of their anger. They often speak in angry terms, complaining about others, and generally have a negative outlook on their life and many of the people and situations in it. The angry reaction, then, is the result of an intellectual and emotional predisposition that they, themselves, set into motion, reacting to the first available opening.

If you feel as though you are reacting quickly in situations, it is a good idea to examine your internal language, what you were experiencing in your daily life, including past traumas and pain (particularly if they remain unresolved), and any current situations that may become exacerbated because you are holding on to anger.

As the opening quote in this chapter suggests, difficult people and situations will continue to show up in your life. An angry reaction may provide immediate relief from your anger and might even the score with your perceived perpetrator, but it does *not* fix your anger; sooner or later, another situation will present itself. It's all about how long you want to remain angry.

## THE 4 KEYS TO REDUCE REACTIVE ANGER

1. Resolve past issues that continue to create present-day anger.
2. Address current life situations that may be producing anxiety and pain.
3. Take action to reduce angry internal thoughts and language.
4. Talk about your anger with someone you trust to create a plan to reduce your anger.

Reactive anger keeps you stuck in an angry disposition and can cause additional problems as you continue to display it. There is one positive about reactive anger: It presents itself quickly and in no uncertain terms; you know you are angry, and you know you have reacted. If this is happening often, it is a tip-off that something is wrong—typically, other sources of anger, either from your past or something currently happening in your life that is unresolved. If this happens only situationally, it is easier to resolve, perhaps requiring nothing more than an apology and taking some simple steps to make sure it does not happen again. On the other hand, if the behavior is constant, it may require additional attention. It is not about evening the score; it is about learning to be happy.

 **TIME TO TAKE ACTION**

1. Unresolved past issues can cause undercurrents of anger that can lie hidden below your emotional surface. It is important to determine if any of these are causing you reactive anger. Talk to someone you trust if you need help with this.

2. If you cannot stop reacting with anger in certain situations or feel the desire to get back at someone or make sure they know you are angry, perhaps there is an undiagnosed physical issue that is contributing to your reactions. (An overactive thyroid can be one such culprit.) Make an appointment with your primary care physician to rule out any contributing health-related factors.

3. If you feel that you cannot control your quick angry reactions to what you think someone has done to you and you cannot slow down enough to give yourself time to examine the facts, it is a good idea to talk to a professional counselor.

## Driving It Home

Reactive anger is often an indication that you either have unresolved underlying issues or something else is happening, perhaps physical or emotional issues. Even though you think your reactive anger successfully evens the score with someone, anger is not working for you; it never does. You may get back at the other person, but you, yourself, must experience the internal anguish that accompanies such an intense reaction. You are worth more than an unrelenting pattern of unrealistic and overwhelming angry reactions. Your life clock is ticking, and you cannot get these moments back. It is time to do what you can to reduce your angry reactions and bring more joy into your life.

**YOUR DECLARATION IS:** *Instead of quickly overreacting in anger, I will learn to examine the facts and respond appropriately!*

## Onward

As you know, anger isn't only a psychological state; it can also have a physical cause. Imbalances in brain chemicals or hormones, low blood sugar, and hormonal issues, for example, can easily give rise to anger, as can other illnesses. The next chapter examines the biological and physiological causes of anger.

CHAPTER 8

# Physiological Anger: It's a Body Thing

*Anger is not simply an intellectual and emotional enterprise; anger often has its roots in the body.*

> **PROCESSES TO EMPLOY:** Brutal Honesty, I Over E, Present/Understand/Fix, Slowing Down Life's Pace, Internal Focus, Fact-Finding, Living in the Moment, Settling Past Issues

ALMOST ANY TIME SOMEONE TALKS ABOUT ANGER, they mention emotional outbursts, how people think angry thoughts, and how angry thoughts can become verbal and behavioral forms of anger. These are, in fact, very important dynamics that relate to anger. However, there is an equally important part of the problem, which has to do with what is happening physically before, during, and after an angry expression. In all preceding books in The Fix Your Empowerment Series, I help readers make the connection between what occurs emotionally/intellectually, spiritually, and what is happening in the body. The goal of this chapter is to help you understand how your body is involved in the way you express anger.

There is a synergistic relationship between your brain, which is charged with the responsibilities of thought and emotion, and your body, which houses the physical processes that keep you alive. The brain and the body are intrinsically interwoven, and together, they are involved in every bodily and neurological process that occurs. For example, the brain either controls the actions or is indirectly involved in every body system. Likewise, the body feeds the brain and nourishes it so that it may continue to be the brilliant intellectual force it is. As I am referring to it in this chapter, "physiological anger" is defined as *the aggressive acceleration process that occurs as the body prepares to engage in battle with another person or object.*

There are two ways the body accelerates to prepare to become angry:

1. **RAPID ACCELERATION:** This occurs when you feel someone has harmed you or you feel threatened, and you react with anger. Little thought is involved in rapid acceleration since the body is responding to an immediate threat. Rapid acceleration quickly prepares you for battle and engages the necessary body systems to accept the challenge. Those systems may include the skeletal system, the muscular system, the cardiovascular system, and the sensory system, especially vision, hearing, and touch. (I will describe these in greater detail shortly.)

2. **DELIBERATE ACCELERATION:** When your body begins the process of deliberate acceleration, you typically have a short interval, say thirty seconds, where you can decide if you want to engage in the battle. In this case, you are deliberately calling on the energy you need for the skirmish. At that point, the same acceleration process occurs as it does with rapid acceleration, but it follows a brief delay and is accompanied by a conscious decision to act aggressively.

Your body accelerates as it prepares for anger because you understand that you are going to need additional resources to engage in battle. Your skeletal system, primarily your bones, gives your body structure. Your body may adjust its posture to give it a more stable base. Your muscles are the other primary anger-delivery system. To strike a blow, you need the sturdiness of your bones as well as the power generated by your muscles.

Since your body is operating at an accelerated pace, the cardiovascular system prepares by making your heart pump faster to deliver more oxygen and blood to your muscles. Increased amounts of oxygen are also applied to the lungs to give you more stamina. Moreover, your eyes will become more intensely focused, your hearing will become more acute, and you will feel more sensitivity and dexterity regarding your sense of touch. Some people also report enhanced sensitivity in their senses of taste and smell, though these are not as important in the delivery of aggressive acts.

## BEFORE, DURING, AND AFTER

As I mentioned earlier, it is important to understand what happens physically before, during, and after an angry expression. Learning about the components of physiological anger gives you a better understanding of how the process of anger develops and how it relates specifically to your circumstances. Another way to look at physiological anger is that the body is getting angry, at times, before the mind understands what is happening. This occurs more prominently in cases of rapid acceleration; however, the more deliberate forms of anger also experience physiological changes. The following is a breakdown of what occurs in each stage as the process develops.

### Before: Preparing for Battle

The best battles are waged when the necessary preparations are made in advance. Regarding the relationship between your body and your mind, anger is processed either rapidly or more deliberately, where there is time to process it intellectually. This means that your brain is involved when you become angry. As discussed in the previous chapter, in cases of rapid-onset anger, your intellectual processes are minimized, but this does not mean they are nonexistent. The brain is *always* involved in what is happening intellectually, physically, and emotionally.

In *The Fix Yourself Handbook*, I examine the psychological phenomenon called habit formation. This is where your brain normalizes thoughts and behaviors that are not typically part of its natural way of functioning. Your brain does its very best to accommodate the way you are living and the decisions you make. If those choices become more routine for you, your brain makes more permanent adjustments. So, if you live life with anger in your daily intellectual and behavioral repertoire, your brain will adjust to this and not only accommodate it but also prepare you for it.

If your brain did not prepare you for those angry outbursts, you would have a more difficult time expressing your anger. But that marvelous thinking machine is always on the job. If you are living with anger as a way to address issues in your relationships or quickly become enraged and behave with aggression, your brain will prepare you for that. If, on the other hand, you are more calm and mild-mannered, your brain will prepare you to live in a more relaxed fashion.

In each case, as your brain and body communicate, preparations are made for the possibility of angry expressions. They keep you ready just in case those scenarios develop. The preparation for battle is your brain and your body communicating to create an efficient way to express your anger. Your brain gets ready for the delivery of an assault, and all your aforementioned physiological systems are readied for action.

Moreover, when your body accelerates and experiences the stress associated with anger, your adrenal glands produce more cortisol, the body's main stress hormone. Cortisol increases your blood pressure and helps your body pump more blood and oxygen to address your body's acceleration. When cortisol is too high, it increases heart rate and blood pressure, triggering negative emotions, and decreases serotonin, the "happy" hormone. The combination of increased blood pressure and reduced serotonin levels can help prepare the body for the acceleration that precedes anger and for the physiological changes that occur when you are angry.

It is important to keep in mind that the primary responsibilities of your brain and body are to do what it takes to keep you alive. Therefore, survival is *always* the foundation of everything you do. I talked about physical and emotional survival in Chapter 3. Both the brain and the body are involved in your survival, so you can expect some communication between them to occur when preparing you for battle, especially since so much of anger is tied to potential threats and assaults on your survival (whether intellectual, emotional, physical, or even spiritual). The physical/intellectual preparation process is a key component in preparing you to become aggressive in threatening situations or when you are simply angry at someone and use anger to settle the score.

## During: In the Battle

When you begin to display anger, especially overt anger, the systems in your body are all on high alert. You are not sure exactly what will happen as the anger progresses, but your mind and your body, working in unison, understand that things have changed and that your body is using resources it typically does not tap into. Think about a time when you became angry. The movement from calm and relaxed to angry and attacking requires pinpoint energy transformation and a body that is ready to access its power as it does its best to annihilate its perceived enemy or, at the very least, disable the threat.

In the previous section, I discuss how the body prepares for battle. There, I examine the various systems in the body and how they prepare for what will happen as you express your anger. During an angry outburst, your body moves from its preparational stage to its battle stage. This is how each of those systems rise to the occasion:

- **THE SKELETAL SYSTEM**: When the battle begins, your skeletal system, having been readied for what may occur, is braced and in protective mode. Your brain understands that an angry outburst could evolve into a physical confrontation, so your skeletal system braces itself to protect your body and its vital organs. In battle, whether it is verbal or physical, your skeletal system is erect, reinforced, and ready to either be on the receiving end of aggression or dish it out.

- **THE MUSCULAR SYSTEM**: Nearly all movement in the body is the result of muscle contraction. In a verbal exchange, your muscles visibly contract and relax, giving you a physical display that lets your adversary know you mean business. In a physical exchange, those contractions and expansions become exaggerated and are designed to grab, push, pull, and strike.

- **THE CARDIOVASCULAR SYSTEM**: In the heat of battle, be it verbal or physical, your body requires more energy, and for that to occur, there is an increased need for blood flow and oxygenation. The heart, lungs, arteries, and veins increase the volume of blood and oxygen to provide increased energy and strength if that becomes necessary.

- **THE SENSORY SYSTEM**: We use our senses to formulate accurate assessments about ourselves, other people, and our environment. Since the brain perceives the threat or you have made a choice to be aggressive, you will experience a moderate to substantial increase in sensory acuity—that is, how efficiently your senses are doing what they should do. In both verbal and physical exchanges, as the physical acceleration process occurs and blood flow is enhanced, your eyes will move faster, and your peripheral vision will be enhanced. Your sense of hearing will search the environment and hone in on any sounds that could be threatening or need to be addressed, and since you may become involved in a physical exchange, your sense of touch and dexterity are enhanced.

## After: When the Battle Ends

Every battle has an endpoint where the body is no longer requiring preparatory and on-demand resources. At this point, each party may have returned to neutral corners, verbal and physical exchanges have ended or are at a bare minimum, and the need for additional physical resources has diminished or ended. There are two stages in this after-the-battle interval, and both are essential for continued health and welfare: 1) rest and relaxation, and 2) recovery.

### *Rest and Relaxation*

After expending a significant amount of energy preparing for and doing battle, the body needs to enter the rest-and-relaxation period, in which it is no longer calling on energy at the accelerated level. This reduction in the need for energy is essential to help you rebound from the stress your body underwent during battle and helps you prepare for a return to normal physiological functioning. Everyone has a normal baseline amount of energy that their body requires. Engaging in angry verbal and physical confrontation demands considerably more energy than your normal baseline level of functioning requires. So, in the rest-and-relaxation period, the amount of energy available to your body dives a bit below your baseline. You may want to sit and relax or even take a nap. Doing so allows your body to restock itself with the energy you need to perform your routine responsibilities.

Since the human body was not designed to stay in fight mode for an extended period, after an extreme expenditure of energy, an *extended* period of relaxation will be required to compensate for the depleted energy reserves. The body strives for homeostasis, the balance that leads to good health. That rapid and accelerated use of energy demanded by an angry exchange requires a period of rest and relaxation to restore balance and refresh your energy storehouse while allowing all the body systems to recover from the trauma they received.

### Recovery

When the body expends energy with acceleration and intensity, the effect is comparable to a physical injury. In each case, during the rest-and-relaxation period, a recovery period must also take place. The skeletal system may have experienced undue stress and, in some cases, fracture. The cardiovascular system needs to return to a normal heartbeat and rate of respiration, and your veins, arteries, and capillaries must relax. The cells in your muscles must regenerate, and the senses need a period of recovery, as they are not intended to operate at such a high level of acuity.

The human body is designed for periods of action followed by periods of rest. Even the most strenuous exercise does not put as much physical demand on the body as the pressure you experience during stressful and accelerated shorter periods of intense anger. Most people do not think about what happens during and after an angry episode as an injurious physical phenomenon. Most of us, however, do understand that after a period of intense exercise, our bodies like to relax. We like to catch our proverbial breath and give our body some time to recover from the strenuous exercise we just experienced. Both strenuous physical exercise and angry outbursts accelerate the body and put stress on all the physical systems. Anger then, just like physical exercise, needs periods of rest, relaxation, and recovery.

## ALL REVVED UP—THE ADRENALINE EFFECT

The hormone adrenaline is secreted by the adrenal glands, especially in conditions of stress. It increases rates of blood circulation, breathing, and carbohydrate metabolism; it also prepares the muscles for exertion. Sometimes, we consciously call on adrenaline to do something that requires more energy to be supplied to the various body systems. Other times, no conscious decision is made. The brain and the body understand that acceleration is being called for, adrenaline is automatically supplied, and you quickly feel energized by this invigorating hormone. This is precisely what happens when you become angry and your body goes into stress mode.

In some cases, like doing low-intensity exercise or walking around the block, you probably won't notice the physical effects of an increase in adrenaline production. However, during periods of high-intensity physical exertion or stress, you may feel stronger, more intense, and more focused, and your physical exertion will be more efficient.

This situational demand for more adrenaline has two primary effects on your body:

1. It provides you with the energy, strength, and other physical resources to accomplish the demands of the task you find yourself in or choose to do.

2. It burns up available physical resources quickly while providing all the additional energy resources you need.

During periods of anger, adrenaline production increases, and as your physiology changes, you will become more intense and supremely prepared for battle. Your bones, muscles, respiration, and senses all become supercharged. Unfortunately, all this energy is being supplied to your body so that you can yell and scream at someone, behave irrationally, break things, and/or possibly do harm to another person.

Again, habit formation allows our brains in conjunction with our bodies to provide what we need in the situations we incorporate into our lives. If it did not supply additional energy at a time when we believe we are under threat, or for our reasons, have chosen to be aggressive, it would be difficult to perform in those situations. So even though your brain is designed to help you survive and do what is right for you in any given situation, sometimes it provides you with the ability to do something that is not necessarily in your best interests.

## KEY TAKEAWAYS

Anger has a physiological component that plays a prominent role in the delivery of aggression, both verbal and physical. Those physical changes prepare us for battle, keep us energized and strong while we are in battle, and help us to recover when the battle has ended. Extreme adrenaline infusion supplies the body with the strength it needs to prevail in potentially threatening situations, but it also uses resources to their maximum capabilities, and the body interprets this as an injurious situation.

**Extremely important:** *Anger may accomplish your goals, but it is never an efficient way to address situations. The wear and tear on your body during periods of anger far outweigh the gains you may receive.*

For some people, anger is a way to a means. It settles scores, lets people know exactly where you stand, provides a brief reactionary interval to frustrating situations, helps you address fearful situations, and can even help you purposefully do damage to another person. With the change in physiology, it is easy to interpret anger as a position of strength. Any martial arts instructor will tell us that real power is rarely, if ever, used. It is the enhanced intellectual capacity that produces the power. Physical exchanges should always be a last resort. As you read on, you will see that this is the case.

## Time to Take Action

1. Continual expressions of anger can have a negative impact on your body. If anger is part of your life, it is a good idea to schedule an appointment with your primary care physician to determine if any physical problems are causing your anger, or if your angry outbursts are causing any physical problems for you.

2. If you experience continued physical acceleration after an angry episode ends, this may be a signal that your body has difficulty entering the rest-and-relaxation stage. Again, speak to your primary care physician about this concern.

3. For some people, the physical reaction to anger supersedes the ability to understand what is happening. Sometimes, it is the rapid increase in adrenaline production that provokes intellectual and emotional reactions. If you feel most of your anger is physically based, it is important to determine if any physical problems caused this to happen. This is one more reason to schedule an appointment with your primary care physician.

4. To avoid the damaging effects of anger, it is a good idea to develop some ways to be more physically relaxed. Breathing exercises, yoga or stretching, prayer, and even physical exercise are good ways to build a calmer approach to circumstances and people in life. You can find primers on breathing exercises and yoga/stretching online.

5. Understand that even though the adrenaline rush and physical prowess that accompanies angry outbursts may make you feel powerful, in the end, your body is not built for this kind of pressure, and your power will be short-lived. Talk about your anger with someone—a friend, a family member, or, if necessary, a professional counselor.

 **DRIVING IT HOME**

Anger is a physical, emotional, and intellectual enterprise. No one becomes angry without some type of physical reaction. Sometimes it begins with fear; sometimes it is a more intellectual episode where someone does something that causes you to think angry thoughts. For others who tend to be more emotional, anger seems to start as an emotional reaction to something. Still, for others, their body engages quickly, and their mind follows. Regardless of the starting point, it is a good idea to learn how to use other options to deal with your anger. Those options are presented in Part Three.

**YOUR DECLARATION IS:** *I will learn about the physical part of my anger to gain better control over my body!*

 **ONWARD**

In an interesting twist, many people believe their anger is necessary and can be productive. In the next chapter, I examine high-minded or righteous anger. I examine why people use it, the flaws in its presentation, and some of the options you can use instead of the high-and-mighty approach.

CHAPTER 9

# Righteous Anger: Anger on the High Road

*Anger "with a cause" will only cause destruction in the end.*

**PROCESSES TO EMPLOY:** Brutal Honesty, I Over E, Present/Understand/Fix, Slowing Down Life's Pace, Internal Focus, Fact-Finding, Faith, Humility, Dignity, Honor, Gratitude, Living in the Moment, Settling Past Issues, Life Inventory

CONSIDERING WHAT I HAVE PRESENTED THUS FAR about anger, it might seem like a stretch to think there is a high road when it comes to using anger in one's life. Some people feel that their way is the right way and that others need to be kept in line if they are doing something unacceptable. These people resort to using anger to manage others, but they believe their anger has a righteous purpose—that is, there is a constructive reason to use it. Anger with a cause is the kind of anger that spurs someone to take action to right a perceived wrong or defend the innocent and the helpless.

Righteous anger is the kind of anger that can fool you into believing that it makes the world a better place. This is anger used by people who believe that others in some way, hurting the world or some part of it, and it is their responsibility to change the thoughts and behaviors of these misguided individuals. This type of anger is condescending, and its users believe they have the right to inflict it on those who are not compliant with their view of the world. Righteous anger, also called righteous indignation, is anger that is primarily motivated by a perception of injustice or another profound moral lapse.

Righteous anger can be misperceived as a positive behavior because it can motivate people to act against injustice and to stand up for what they believe is right. People who use righteous anger often search for injustices perpetrated by individuals, large companies, and governments. When they identify what they believe are personal or social wrongdoings, they use angry outbursts to draw attention to what they believe are the unjust behaviors of others. For our purposes, I am defining "righteous anger" as *the belief that the thoughts and behavior of others are unjust, and must, in no uncertain terms, be dealt with accordingly.*

Here are some examples of righteous anger:

- Violence to protest social injustices.
- Anger directed toward children and family members to "set them on the right course."
- Verbally attacking someone who seems boastful about the abundance in their life.
- Verbal assaults on others who have broken the law or hurt other people.
- Politicians who attack their opponent for some perceived moral or illegal action.
- Attacks against other people whose opinions differ from those of the person using the anger.

## THE NOT-SO-HIGH HIGH ROAD

The use of righteous anger assumes that the user is moral and above the unethical, illegal, abusive, or evil behaviors of another person. It seeks to draw attention to someone else's decisions or mistakes, publicly exposing them and verbally or physically attacking them. A person using righteous anger has intellectualized their use of an abusive response to someone's actions, making it look like the expression of anger is not only beneficial but necessary to right the wrong the other person committed.

It is important to keep in mind that regardless of how it is expressed or the reasons to express it, anger is always packed with negative energy. It can never be used to garner positive results. *Negative energy always yields negative results.* There is the old way of thinking that says constructive criticism can be a positive thing. That is only true when it is expressed with a warm approach, with the feelings of the other person in mind, and when the user also expresses warm acceptance for the other person on other occasions. The use of any form of anger as a method to right social evils or set people on the right course will rarely, if ever, yield positive results.

People who use righteous anger firmly believe they are, in fact, righteous. The traditional definition of "righteous" *is a person or conduct morally right or justifiable, virtuous.* This is where righteous anger differs from the other types of anger. When a person using other types of anger is expressing anger to another person, concerns about being virtuous or morally correct rarely enter the argument. Someone does something or you perceive they did, and you react accordingly. You are angry and usually not giving much thought to how you are thinking or behaving, at least not in terms of morality or virtue.

Those who use righteous anger assume that they are morally, spiritually, or socially above the target of their anger. That person has somehow violated a moral or sacred principle and clearly needs to be punished. Using anger, in this case, feels justified because the person using it firmly believes the other person deserves their wrath and that it is beneficial in a big-picture way. We often see righteous anger used by people trying to alter the social climate to fit their needs. When this doesn't happen, they perceive the actions of the target of their anger as so deplorable that any attempt to communicate with them will not work; therefore, they believe that anger is all a wretched person can understand.

# THE FLY IN THE RIGHTEOUS OINTMENT

Being moral demands that people act morally. To be moral demands three basic components: moral reasoning, moral emotions, and proper conduct. This means one must think, emote, and behave according to higher principles and moral conduct. The question is, how is using anger in any situation and with anyone a moral act? In Chapter 1, I defined "anger" as *an aggressive physical, emotional, and intellectual strategy or response to people, places, and things in our lives that has a negative impact on our lives and the lives of those close to us.* So, the flaw in the reasoning of the person using righteous anger is that using anger will not produce negative results. Once again, *Negative energy always yields negative results.* It has a greater potential to hurt the target of the anger and it will also hurt the person using it.

The human mind has an interesting way of intellectualizing information, so its presentation looks intelligent, even when it is not. We generally tend to convince ourselves that we are right and others are wrong or that we are moral and they are not. We can talk ourselves into believing that we are doing the right thing when we decide to use anger to attack another in the name of restoring justice or righting someone else's sinking ship. It is interesting to note that the formula we use to correct those purveyors of injustice is one that utilizes verbal abuse, negative affirmations, and at times, physical violence. Talk about the pot calling the kettle black.

Those who use righteous anger are often people who feel the need to call attention to themselves as members of higher status in the social order. This decision may come from one or more of the following:

1. Someone may need attention, and publicly chastising another individual creates that spotlight for them.
2. Some people feel as though their opinion is the correct one and will use degrading tactics to make it look like others are unjust. They need to be right and need others to know they are.

3. In cases where someone has been victimized, righteous anger is a safer way to settle the score with unjust bullies than facing past demons head-on.

4. At times, righteous anger has a big-picture plan. It can be used to further the personal, professional, or social agenda of the person using it.

5. To vilify others as being wrong or unjust, knowing that your own agenda is unjust, and attacking them before that they can draw negative attention to what you are doing.

## CROWD-PLEASING

Righteous anger emanates from a place deep inside you where you firmly believe that you are moral and righteous. This creates a judgmental way of thinking, and you may actively look for some immoral or unjust behavior. Righteous anger is often applied in situations like defending a perceived victim or selecting a segment of the population you feel is being victimized by those in power. The interesting dynamic regarding righteous anger is that it is almost always expressed in the public view.

Take the examples of two people who attend church services every week. One of those people maintains their humility, has their primary focus on their faith, and enjoys fellowship with other members of the congregation. They rarely, if ever, have anything negative to say about anyone else. They have been taught the fine points of spirituality and live by them. The second person likes to be seen at church. They know the writings associated with their religion and can often recite them verbatim. They believe that by spouting all the laws and other rules of their religion, others will see them as spiritual people. They, however, are usually the people condemning others and verbally doing their best to cast them into the anti-spiritual abyss.

Another example is the person who publicly attempts to identify with some social movement, never really being a part of that movement. They will do their best to attract attention to themselves if they overindulge in the popularized mission of that social movement, but they are never fully invested in it. So that they may appear to be part of that intensely demanded social change, they launch heated attacks at people with opposing points of view and do it using a public platform, all the time attempting to present themselves as righteous, justified, and taking the social high road.

Very few people who practice humility and have a high moral code need others to believe they are righteous people. That is a personal matter they address in their lives each day by thinking and behaving according to a moral and dignified code. Conversely, righteous anger, needing its external audience, attempts to create a separation between the aggressor and their victims. Here's the interesting twist: People who practice righteous anger often do so for those social injustices where they are publicly defending other people or intensely representing some social cause. In each case, victimization is the foundation of their attack. However, *while they are busy attacking other people, they are creating new victims*. Isn't that what they are fighting against?

People who use righteous anger never really take the high road. They are usually not concerned with what happens to the targets of their aggression. They have decided that their position is the moral and socially correct position and typically do not do the research necessary to understand what the other person or people are doing. Rather, they attack based on small sample sizes of information. They are so intent on attracting attention to their cause that they find it difficult to take the time to gather the facts necessary to make intelligent decisions. As a result, they never really change anything and may inflict considerable pain on others. Also, it usually doesn't take long for others to realize that their actions are for public display, and people eventually stop listening to them. Taking a step back, getting the facts, and treating others with respect would go a long way instead of using anger, while it has the added advantage of mutual respect.

## THE HIGH ROAD, REVISED

It is not often that people who use righteous anger see positive results from their methods. Since the vehicle to expose other people's wrongdoings is anger, the possibility of realizing any positive results is significantly minimized. Also, if the person using righteous anger obtained the positive results they were seeking, there would be no need to continue being angry, but that was never the reason to use this sinister tool in the first place. The underlying goal of righteous anger is to convince others that you are righteous.

Righteous anger is an example of using anger for profit. In Chapter 12, I will discuss some more about profiteering using anger as a strategic tool. Specifically, the person using righteous anger wants to enhance their social and moral standing in the community. This is not to say that the causes they attach themselves to are not worthwhile ventures. Many of them are. The concern is that, once again, they are using negative, abusive, and sometimes violent methods to expose the dark side of other people, as they see it.

In anything we do, there is doing it to achieve a goal, and there is doing it to fulfill a personal need. Often, any gains that could be realized by using righteous anger never really come to fruition. People using righteous anger tend to use it because they need to. They need to be heard, to feel as though they are better than others, and to convince themselves that they are moral and committed to a cause. They need to convince themselves that they are strong. There is nothing wrong with committing oneself to positive change, but positive gains are usually the result of positive methodologies. Stripped down to its core elements, righteous anger is still anger—nothing more. It would be far more productive to use positive means to instigate change than methods that can inflict pain and harm others.

The advice here is simple: Instead of deciding that you are taking the high road and behaving in a righteous, moral fashion by using an abusive tool like righteous anger to achieve your goals, it makes more sense to be positive and diplomatic in your approach. Make sure you have all the information about the person or cause you have decided to involve yourself with. Righteous anger is reactive and rarely has the facts. Make sure that in all you do, fact-finding proceeds any judgments and actions you may take in your dealings with others. Think about warm communication instead of righteous indignation. Never feel as though you are more righteous and have higher standards than anyone else. Doing so is often the first step in avoiding the not-so-righteous abyss.

The next time you feel as though you want to verbally attack or be aggressive toward someone because you think you have all the answers, it makes good sense to take a step back and ask yourself why you believe you need to take such measures against that person. Sometimes being right doesn't tell the whole story. Regardless of how moral you are and how right you think you are, you have chosen to use anger to attack a fellow human being. There is no faster way to fall from the grace of the high road than by attempting to hurt others. Take a good look at this one.

 **TIME TO TAKE ACTION**

1. Ask yourself if you feel you are more righteous than the people you are attacking. If your answer is yes, you may have convinced yourself that using anger is the right decision to make. Answering this requires brutal honesty.

2. Take a hard look at anyone you may have used righteous anger to hurt. Is there another method you could have used to address this situation?

3. If you can, try to determine how your anger progressed from righteous thoughts to the point of verbal or physical attacks.

4. List how often you either use righteous anger or think about doing so. Again, be honest with yourself.

5. Discuss how you have used or may be using righteous anger with someone you trust. Try not to make this a person who is also involved in your cause. Get a fresh perspective on the methods you use and why you use them.

**6.** If you feel that the use of righteous anger stems from some unresolved past issues or insecurities you are currently feeling, it makes good sense to discuss these with a professional counselor.

 ## DRIVING IT HOME

There are many ways to address issues and deal with people we feel are making decisions or doing things that can cause problems for others. Not everyone runs their life using a moral compass. It is important not to be drawn into an angry battle that we believe is justified by hiding it behind a moral or righteous mask. Regardless of what you use anger to accomplish, it is still anger, it is still negative, and it still hurts the person to whom you are directing the anger as well as yourself. Do take the high road, but do it without causing someone else pain and without putting yourself in a position to rely on a tool that can only bring pain into your life.

**YOUR DECLARATION IS:** *I will never make my anger look like it is a productive way to live. I will be positive in my approach with myself and others!*

 ## ONWARD

There is an anger that doesn't express itself as overt anger. Instead, it seeps out in little ways, such as sarcastic comments or acts of hidden aggression against others. In the next chapter, I examine passive-aggressive anger, the damage it does, and how to avoid using this sneaky little tool.

CHAPTER 10

# Passive-Aggressive Anger: The Secret Punisher

*Passive-aggressiveness is anger's most efficient lie. It says, "I am not angry" before it attacks.*

**PROCESSES TO EMPLOY:** Brutal Honesty, I Over E, Present/Understand/Fix, Slowing Down Life's Pace, Internal Focus, Fact-Finding, Living in the Moment, Settling Past Issues, Life Inventory

**THE EXPRESSION OF ANGER ISN'T ALWAYS AN** in-your-face verbal or physical explosion. Not everyone is comfortable with exaggerated emotional confrontations, and some people prefer to express their anger subtly without the possibility of a volatile backlash. For some, it is easier to make a stand by doing almost nothing at all: instead of holding firm against something, they stand back. Though they may feel hurt by another's actions, they do not overtly express their anger. They prefer to use more passive tactics to make their point.

Anger seeps out in little ways, such as sarcastic comments or acts of unconscious or conscious aggression against the person you are mad at, such as "forgetting" to gas up the car when you know your partner won't have enough gas to make it to work the next morning. Using the silent treatment to let someone know you are angry and being unwilling to give them any information about what occurred to make you angry also works. For some, passive-aggressive anger can be expressed and run its course in a few hours. For others, it may take several days or even weeks before the anger subsides.

In addition to the above examples, passive-aggressive anger can also be expressed thusly:

- **BACKHANDED COMPLIMENTS**: A seemingly pleasant remark about someone that can also be an insult.
- **SARCASM**: Using words that mean the opposite of what you really want to say, especially to insult someone, show irritation, or get laughs.
- **BLAMING OTHERS**: Instead of directly confronting the wrongdoing, others may receive blame for something not connected to the original problem.
- **INEFFICIENT OR INCOMPLETE TASKS**: Getting back at someone with whom you are angry by leaving tasks half done or making them wait because it will cause problems for that person.
- **SABOTAGING OTHERS**: Deliberately destroying or damaging something or obstructing someone from doing something.
- **PROCRASTINATING**: Saying that you will do something but making others wait.
- **WITHHOLDING COMPLIMENTS**: Purposely and clearly not paying any attention to someone's success or other accomplishment.
- **CREATING A TENSE SITUATION**: Being so tense that others either avoid you or are very careful not to say or do anything around you that might provoke your ire.
- **MAKING EXCUSES**: Purposely not doing something that is expected of you and then making excuses that the other person clearly knows are not valid.
- **CRITICIZING INDIRECTLY**: Making a comment that could be taken as criticism but does not overtly criticize the other person.
- **BEING STUBBORN**: Not accepting suggestions, being uncooperative, and refusing to compromise your point of view.
- **DENYING ANGER**: Insisting you are not angry even though it is clear to the other person that you are.

## THE UNRELENTING SCOREKEEPER

Common among all users of passive-aggressive anger is a well-developed talent for keeping score. These people forget nothing. In fact, those who are passive-aggressive look for comments and behaviors to add to their list of items to react to. It is not uncommon to hear a litany of complaints and unresolved victimization when someone who is passive-aggressive finally expresses what is on their mind. This is because instead of confronting a problem when it occurs and attempting to arrive at a compromise or a solution, they hold on to almost everything that happens. This is how the passive-aggressive strategy develops; nothing ever gets resolved.

Almost all passive-aggressive people have difficulty confronting unsettling situations. They are often fearful and concerned about the other person's response, which they assume will be angry or confrontive. Because they have difficulty in emotionally charged situations, this causes them to avoid what could be a productive conversation. Instead, they attempt to let the other person know they are angry without ever really telling them the reason for the anger. Meanwhile, they obsess over what occurred, which fuels their anger and encourages their passive-aggressive behavior.

Most passive-aggressive people are obsessive thinkers, which means it is difficult for them to stop thinking about something—especially if it is emotionally charged. This places them in a position to feel victimized. Without a way to stop the obsessive thoughts, the person searches for relief, turning to indirect or passive ways to get their anger across and hoping the other person gets the message and changes their behavior or opens a dialogue (but see the next discussion).

## MAKING MATTERS WORSE

If the recipient of the anger tries to open a dialogue, the passive-aggressive person will likely respond by saying nothing is wrong, exacerbating the problem. Even though the situation is now on the table for discussion, the passive-aggressive person continues to avoid the subject, stubbornly refusing to communicate. This usually results in the other person giving up with no resolution, and the anger-provoking situation continues. Now, the passive-aggressive person will either withdraw from the situation or become angrier. This is when the angry person's behavior might escalate, and they may do something to the other person that is more visible. Perhaps they hide some of their possessions or maybe even destroy them. They may escalate from no communication whatsoever to angry outbursts that are off-target—that is, they do not communicate anything about the original problem.

Passive-aggressive people don't just become passive-aggressive later in their lives. They have usually had a long-standing difficulty communicating their feelings of victimization or about situations they perceive as unfair. So, consequently, as their life progresses, they will have had a long history of internal victimization without resolution. A new wrongdoing against them merely attaches to what is already there, and the same behavior is repeated, again without resolution.

## TURNING INWARD

As the unresolved anger continues to develop, passive-aggressive people can use their strategies to convince themselves they are not angry. There is an arrogance attached to passive aggression that does not allow the person using it to admit that they are angry and that the other person has that much control over them. They do their best to convince others and themselves that they will not be victimized by what they feel the other person has done to them. In many cases, after continued passive-aggressive standoffs, the other person is no longer reacting to the passive aggression since they are routinely told that nothing is wrong. Still, the passive-aggressive abuse continues. The person using it can become frustrated that their tactics have been unsuccessful, and without understanding what is happening, they may turn their aggression inward.

When this happens, the person who has exhausted passive-aggressive strategies on others may begin to use those methods on themselves, sometimes consciously and sometimes unconsciously. Remember, this is an obsessive condition, and the person using passive aggression cannot stop thinking about it. Since other people are no longer responding to their strategy, the person begins to do things that may be hurtful to themselves in an attempt to convince others that they are in pain without admitting that they are. The hope is that other people will see them hurting themselves and attempt to stop it. Unfortunately, if people do attempt to address this self-deprecating behavior, the passive aggressor will again simply say that nothing is wrong, and the abusive cycle continues. Some of the self-deprecating behaviors that may result are:

- Stress eating
- Alcohol or drug abuse
- Excessive shopping
- Behaving erratically
- Temper tantrums
- Panic attacks
- Self-harm such as cutting, hitting, and burning oneself
- Suicide attempts

For people who have difficulty communicating with others and expressing concern when they feel someone has violated their rights or offended them, confrontations can be overwhelming and produce serious anxiety. The very thought of having to confront someone they feel has done something wrong to them can create symptoms ranging from mild anxiety to panic. Not all passive-aggressive people are purposefully trying to hurt others. In a very confused way to solve a problem, they are trying to get attention, hoping the situation can be resolved without confrontation.

Often, people who use passive aggression have a poor self-image and do not believe they are deserving of the changes they are hoping for. It is not uncommon for them to have been routinely invalidated and to hear that their complaints are irrelevant and minuscule. When they do approach others, they do it without confidence and often ask for forgiveness before they express what is concerning them.

Here is an example of what happens when a person who uses passive-aggressive anger has a concern that needs to be addressed:

Marsha is a forty-eight-year-old mother of three. She has been married to Justin for twenty years. She works in the finance department at the local bank where she is well respected. Marsha and Justin have a good relationship, but there are times when he can be inconsiderate and not pay attention to her needs or her boundaries. Marsha grew up in a family where the expression of feelings and concerns was discouraged, and she is not sure how to efficiently confront Justin when he does something that hurts her feelings.

Justin has some communication issues and can overreact in certain situations. When he does this, Marsha reacts by avoiding the situation, so her concerns are rarely validated. Since Marsha cannot efficiently communicate her feelings to her husband, she compensates by giving him the silent treatment and answering him with curt responses. At times, she will hide something he is looking for or sabotage something important to him. She is desperately trying to get his attention so that he will understand what she is feeling, but Justin has absolutely no idea why Marsha behaves as she does.

This is an example of what happens when someone who has difficulty with communication finds themselves in a position where they need to confront someone on an issue that is important to them. If Marsha could communicate to Justin what is bothering her, she could avoid all the passive-aggressive behavior she is using. While Justin may or may not agree with her, the most important issue is that Marsha no longer feels unworthy of expressing herself and will not have to resort to clandestine behaviors to get her husband's attention.

## GIVE IT TO ME STRAIGHT

If we don't communicate what is on our mind and what we will and will not accept from others, people will inevitably violate our boundaries and behave inconsiderately, seemingly without any concern for the way we think or feel. We cannot expect others to routinely understand how we think and feel and comply with how we would like things to be done. We all have our own ideas about how we would like others to respect and understand us. However, no one can fully understand our wishes until we communicate them in an understandable way.

The most efficient way to confront anyone is to present them with the facts. This should be done without accusations, anger, and negative emotional outbursts. The goal should be to help those with whom we share space to understand what is important to us and what we are hoping for from them. This does not ensure they will cooperate with our wishes, but it does help reduce (and possibly remove) the need for passive-aggressive thoughts and actions. It also reduces those overwhelming obsessive thoughts that can cause so much pain.

## THE 5 KEYS TO EFFICIENT CONFRONTATION

1. Try to obtain the other person's undivided attention and their willingness to hear what you have to say. For instance, you can ask, "May I please have a moment of your time? I would like to talk about something."

2. Keep emotions at a minimum and stay on point. Take some time to think about what you want to say before you start the conversation. Go into the conversation as relaxed as you can.

3. Provide the facts clearly so they can understand what is important to you.

4. Allow the other person to respond to what you are saying. Make it a dialogue, not a lecture.

5. Be willing to compromise to arrive at a solution.

If the person you are attempting to communicate with is unwilling to discuss the situation with you, let them know how you feel about this, calmly. You can even say that you are not willing to do anything in the relationship until this matter is discussed. Doing this allows you to make the attempt to communicate, but also sets boundaries with regard to what will occur should they not give you the consideration you deserve. At this point, as you may notice, you no longer held the matter inside. They know that there is a problem, and exactly what they need to do to address the situation.

No one likes to be put in a position where they must confront someone about undesirable behavior. It creates anxiety and fear, and there is always the concern that the conversation may escalate to an unfriendly level. We cannot control other people's responses and actions, but we *can* control what we do. Though you may find it uncomfortable to confront someone, not doing so puts you in a position to obsess over your concerns and you may find yourself performing those confusing clandestine behaviors, which, in the end, can only cause more problems for you.

 **TIME TO TAKE ACTION**

1. Rather than rely on passive-aggressive behavior, if someone crosses your boundaries and you would like them to stop this behavior, discuss the situation with another person with whom you feel close to help you gain clarity and organize the facts about the situation.

2. Use the "5 Keys to Efficient Confrontation." Once you are clear on all the facts, ask the person whose behavior you would like to stop to talk about it with you. Present just the facts and keep your emotions to a minimum. Try to make it a discussion rather than an accusatory discourse. Give the other person time to say what is on their mind. Attempt to arrive at a solution and be prepared to compromise.

3. If they refuse to discuss the situation, let them know that you attempted to warmly discuss it, and that you are unwilling to do anything else until the matter is resolved.

4. If you feel as though the matter could become angry or violent, step away, share what has happened with a friend or family member, and together, try to decide on a plausible direction to address your situation.

5. If you continue to have problems communicating and find yourself resorting to passive-aggressive tactics, this default behavior may be related to past issues. Also, if there is a fear of aggression or violence you may need considerably more help. Talking to someone such as a professional counselor about your difficulties in this regard can help.

 **DRIVING IT HOME**

Passive-aggressive anger is usually the result of unresolved issues. Those issues may be confined to your present circumstances, or this behavior may be in response to long-standing communication issues or past pain and trauma. Do your best to communicate your feelings with those close to you. Your opinions and concerns are important, and you do have the right to express them. If you are having trouble making the initial attempt, or you have made attempts that either go nowhere or make the situation worse, it may be time to talk it over with a counselor to help you understand what is happening in your life and why. Put a stop to passive-aggressive anger and learn to become a person who can communicate what is important to you.

**YOUR DECLARATION IS:** *I will learn to confront others peacefully to free myself of obsessive thoughts and passive-aggressive anger!*

 **ONWARD**

Sometimes anger can escalate to the point where it can strike fast and hard. In the next chapter, I examine how volatile anger works, how difficult it is to control, and the consequences of expressing it in one's life. I will also provide you with the necessary advice to overcome anger when it becomes volatile.

CHAPTER 11

# Volatile Anger: Blowing Your Stack

*You think quick, strike fast, and annihilate the enemy, but in the end, you are both predator and prey.*

**PROCESSES TO EMPLOY:** Brutal Honesty, I Over E, Present/Understand/Fix, Slowing Down Life's Pace, Internal Focus, Fact-Finding, Living in the Moment, Settling Past Issues, Life Inventory

VOLATILE ANGER IS THE ANTITHESIS OF PASSIVE-AGGRESSIVE anger. Sometimes called intermittent explosive anger, volatile anger erupts quickly, and there is little if any control on the user's part. This type of anger involves repeated sudden bouts of impulsive, aggressive, violent behavior, or angry verbal outbursts. The reactions are often far too extreme for the situation. These explosive outbursts may only occur intermittently but can cause major damage to the objects of the anger. These angry eruptions can harm relationships and cause serious problems at work or school. Many people who experience volatile anger find themselves in trouble with the legal system. Road rage, throwing or breaking objects, and severe temper tantrums may be symptoms of volatile anger.

This kind of anger is often unpredictable. It can easily spiral out of control, leading to words and actions you immediately regret once the storm has passed, but may leave a lasting effect on the targets of the anger. When your anger becomes volatile, you know you are mad and so does everyone else. However, it is very difficult to stop being angry once it starts. This anger is often seen as impulsive and sometimes unprovoked. It can last for just a few minutes or as long as thirty minutes. For some, volatile anger is expressed often, but for most people, there is a reasonable period between outbursts, at times, it could be a month or two. In some cases, verbal outbursts or less severe physical attacks may still occur in between displays of volatile anger.

Most people who display volatile anger can be irritable, impulsive, aggressive, or angry most of the time. Triggers of volatile anger can include a situation, an individual, a personal issue, or past trauma. In addition, substance abuse is frequently a contributing factor in volatile anger. For some, displays of volatile anger date back to their formative years. Risk factors that can trigger volatile anger include living environments, genetics, and a history of mental illness.

Though the onset of volatile anger seems to be fast and furious, the person experiencing it is not instantaneously transitioning from calm and peaceful to angry and irate. In Chapter 5, I discussed undercurrents of unresolved past pain and trauma that can lead to angry expressions. People who have volatile anger usually have those undercurrents, some of which could be physical (e.g., thyroid or hormonal issues, high blood pressure, or chronic pain), some of which could be emotional (e.g., past traumas and abuse), and some of which could be intellectual (e.g., obsessive thoughts). These undercurrents set the stage for the angry volatile episode.

## SETTING THINGS UP

Because these undercurrents keep the volatile, angry person primed to act out, their anger meter is already running high. Quite often, they feel like nothing goes right for them. Little things set them off because they are already dealing with angry undercurrents from past pain and traumas, and there simply isn't enough intellectual/

emotional space to rationally process new events. So, on the turn of a dime, it seems as though they lose control and go into a rage. This intense onset of anger gives the impression that they might explode at any moment, so others do their best to either placate them or avoid them altogether.

Before an aggressive bout, a volatile person may:

- **FEEL IRRITABLE**: They may be easily annoyed or become angry.

- **BE MORE TENSE AND ENERGETIC**: They have difficulty relaxing and always seem to have an abundance of energy.

- **HAVE RACING THOUGHTS**: It is difficult for them to stop thinking, and they are often dealing with many thoughts simultaneously.

- **EXPERIENCE BODY TINGLING**: Since the nervous system is operating at a heightened level, they may feel tingling, primarily in their extremities.

- **START SHAKING**: With the nervous system sensitized, it is not uncommon for them to experience shaking and muscle contractions.

- **HAVE A FAST OR POUNDING HEARTBEAT**: The accelerated neurological pace causes an increase in heart rate, which ranges from a slight acceleration to heavy pounding.

- **EXPERIENCE CHEST TIGHTNESS**: As the heart continues to work harder, they may feel tightness in the chest.

- **HAVE A PANIC ATTACK**: The acceleration often causes acute anxiety, which may develop into a panic attack that can range from mild to quite severe.

- **BE IN THE INITIAL STAGES OF RAGE**: Before going into a full-blown volatile angry episode, there are initial stages of rage that can include hyperactivity, cursing, intense pacing, and verbal abuse.

## SELF-MEDICATION

For some people, experiencing all these symptoms leads to misguided attempts to medicate the problem. Self-medication rarely, if ever, begins as a result of a visit with one's primary care physician. This is something people choose to do without professional advice. It can have the advantage of soothing irritability, reducing the impact of racing thoughts, and reducing the intensity of tension and anxiety. The problem is that self-prescribed medications do not possess the ability to address the cause of the problem, so repeated doses are always necessary. The other downside of self-medicating is the possibility of dependence on the drug, and all too often, the drugs selected by the person experiencing the symptoms lead to other problems such as relationship issues, employment problems, and/or physical issues.

It is also important to keep in mind that many of these self-administered medications can exacerbate the undercurrents and enhance the possibility of volatile outbursts. Alcohol is one of the drugs most often selected by those who experience volatile anger. The abovementioned symptoms often have the person searching for a quick way to relieve the agony. Alcohol acts quickly, but consistent with so many drugs, the body builds tolerance to it, and larger doses are required. This can lead to alcohol-induced volatile episodes, and since there can be a marked physical/emotional/intellectual impact, some of the undercurrents become worse.

Another problem with self-medicating is that an agitated person's body is already experiencing the effects of heightened neurological activity and physical stress. Though alcohol and other drugs may relieve the symptoms initially, they also place undue stress on the body, and the recovery period becomes difficult due to the physical withdrawal. Withdrawal is often thought of as an acute reaction where a person becomes sick, experiences sweat and tremors, vomits, and may need a day or two in bed. The milder form of withdrawal includes minor physical symptoms like headache, upset stomach, and tiredness, which can increase intolerance, irritability, and anger.

Volatile people can quickly gain a reputation for being difficult, quick-tempered, abusive, and at times, dangerous. This has much to do with what people see as volatile people explode and from witnessing their volatile tirades. They can also earn their reputation since the undercurrents of their anger are continuously expressed. If they are not demonstrating anger, they are either poised to do so or constantly seem to be irritable and difficult to deal with. It is important to note that people who demonstrate volatile anger are also unhappy, in conflict, and struggling both intellectually and emotionally. They are routinely experiencing mood swings, and internally, they are reacting even when they are not displaying their anger. They have little to no control over their moods and how they feel emotionally.

Intellectually, their minds never shut off. Mentally, they run through one angry scenario after another, and there seems to be no permanent resolutions to any of the issues that plague their minds. Outwardly, they are doing little more than displaying what they are feeling on the inside. Physical acceleration, emotional instability, and intellectual conflict permeate their lives. There are times when the angry outbursts are a cry for help, but neither the volatile person nor anyone in their purview would believe this to be the case. They are angry, they can be mean and in-your-face, and if pushed, their behavior is unpredictable and may be dangerous.

## WE HAVE LIFTOFF

You can liken an angry person's volatile outburst to a lid on a pot of boiling water over high heat. Always at a high simmer, it is only a matter of time until the lid blows. When the lid does blow—that is, when the angry person becomes volatile—anyone who is nearby goes into self-protect mode. There isn't a lot of time to try to analyze the situation and understand what this angry person is feeling. Though their reputation may have been earned, it is difficult for others to understand why they behave the way they do. Since they are so difficult to approach, helping them seems like an impossible task.

Once the volatile outburst begins, the angry person has little to no control over themselves. There is also no way to tell how long it will last or how intense it will become. There does not need to be a monumental reason for the explosion. Oftentimes, others cannot detect a visible reason for the outburst. The explosive verbal and behavioral demonstrations are much too intense for the situation, and the person gives no thought to what might happen because of their blowup. During the tirade, collateral damage never enters their mind. Again, control over themselves seems to have been compromised; the angry person is on autopilot. Their mental faculties seem disconnected, and their anger is in full control of their thoughts and actions.

Volatile outbursts can include:

- **TEMPER TANTRUMS**: These can range from whining and crying to screaming, kicking, hitting, and even breath-holding.

- **LONG, ANGRY SPEECHES**: Here, the person goes on a verbal tirade about anything and everything they feel others have done to them or how the world is not fair to them.

- **SHOUTING**: An elevated voice goes hand in hand with volatile anger. Every reaction is elevated. They will talk at and over people. They will scream to make their point if they must.

- **THREATS**: They may threaten to do something to the other person or their property; they may also threaten to harm themselves.

- **PROPERTY DAMAGE**: This includes breaking inanimate objects, tools, and anything within arm's reach.

- **HEATED ARGUMENTS**: There is no reasoning with a volatile person. Their minds have been overtaken by anger, and they cannot process information coherently. They will argue back, often irrationally, and usually cover the same ground repeatedly.

- **SLAPPING, SHOVING, OR PUSHING AND PHYSICAL FIGHTS**: If the anger becomes exacerbated, it is not out of the question for them to physically attack another person, with behaviors ranging from mild pushes to shoves, slaps, and at times punches where the out-of-control intent is to harm the other person.

# THE SHUTDOWN

Volatile anger is an incredibly demanding and often excruciating way to live. Volatile outbursts demand an extreme amount of energy, and there is a tremendous amount of temporary damage done to the body, emotions, and mind. Physically, every system in the body tightens and experiences the acceleration concomitant with the volatile outburst. Emotionally, the mood swing is so intense that the emotions take over the intellect and feed on the body's overproduction of adrenaline. Emotional instability uses a vast amount of energy and can leave the body feeling broken and exhausted. Intellectually, the mind experiences intense conflict and is flooded with information at a rate it cannot process.

Though the volatile mind may have done its best to tear down its victim, the angry person walks away broken and battered. As adrenaline production begins to return to normal, it is not uncommon to feel muscular pain and exhaustion to the point that rest is essential. At times, following the volatile outburst, calming drugs like alcohol, marijuana, and pharmaceuticals may be used to help promote a return to homeostasis and physical/emotional/intellectual stability.

This is often where the angry person has an opportunity to examine the damage they have done. Now, with their intellect processing information with more clarity and emotions being expressed at a more stable level, they can see the damage they have done to others and perhaps property. Some will be apologetic and remorseful, and they will do what they can to fix the situation. Depending on their mental health and how severe the undercurrent is, others may insist they were right, though they may agree they didn't need to take it as far as they did.

If your anger rises to the point where it becomes volatile, it makes sense to schedule an appointment with your primary care physician. Physical issues are often involved in some cases of volatile anger, and your doctor will arrange for blood work to determine if everything is normal. They will also perform an in-office examination to ensure that the anger is not physically instigated. Your physician may suggest that you check in with a professional counselor to deal with your anger and any undercurrents that may be part of the problem.

No one should use anger to address situations in their life, and even more importantly, no one should have to live life in danger of hurting themselves or those close to them. If your anger has progressed to this point, it is a good idea to take action to remedy this behavior before you or someone else is seriously injured.

 **TIME TO TAKE ACTION**

1. There is no "maybe" with volatile anger. If you have it, you know it and so does everyone else. Make an appointment with your primary care physician to get started on your healing journey.

2. Because of the intense physical/emotional/intellectual acceleration you were experiencing, your memory of events may not be accurate. Be willing to listen to those who are close to you and have witnessed your volatile outbursts; their reports of what happened will likely be more accurate than yours.

3. Try not to be defensive when others approach you about using this type of anger. There is no rational reason to use it, and if you did, and cannot stop, you need help. If you cannot stop using this type of anger on your own, be willing to get the help you need.

4. Volatile anger has a deep connection to undercurrents that may stem from unresolved past issues. If you have this type of anger, contact a professional counselor. They can help you sort through those issues and anything else that may be causing your volatility.

 **DRIVING IT HOME**

Volatile anger does not take much to diagnose. If you have it, you are losing control, throwing tantrums, breaking things, and hurting other people. These actions are readily observable. Try not to deny what is happening in your life. You may not mean to be so angry and possibly so dangerous. However, when things escalate, you are out of control and are not always holding yourself accountable for what is happening during those outbursts. Before you hurt yourself or anyone else, get help for this. See your primary care physician and a professional counselor. Settle the issues that may be causing such intense anger. If you do, you will be more at peace with yourself and others.

**YOUR DECLARATION IS:** *I will take the necessary steps to reduce my volatile anger and become more peaceful with myself and others!*

 **ONWARD**

The human mind can learn to understand that other people's responses to our anger can make us feel powerful and more in control. In the next chapter, I examine how anger can be used to manipulate other people and for personal profit.

# CHAPTER 12

# Anger for Profit: Aggressive Control

*Beware of using anger as a tool of manipulation. You may get what you want but only at a high cost to your spirit.*

**PROCESSES TO EMPLOY:** Brutal Honesty, I Over E, Present/Understand/Fix, Slowing Down Life's Pace, Internal Focus, Fact-Finding, Living in the Moment, Settling Past Issues, Life Inventory

**SO FAR WE HAVE LOOKED AT ANGER** through various lenses, including as a reaction to someone's words or actions, as a physical problem, and as the result of unresolved issues. I have not yet placed the spotlight directly on using anger strategically. In cases like passive-aggressive anger and righteous anger, some thought is being applied to how anger is expressed and may be perceived by others, but anger for profit is an entirely different way to use anger.

As I have stressed throughout this book, the human brain is a highly adaptive thinking machine. For us to survive, we must extrapolate information from our experiences and our environment to keep us alive and safe. But this marvelous human brain also learns how to be strategic. It learns how to get ahead. It takes the notion of survival of the fittest and repackages it as power of the cleverest. It is to the winner go the spoils. This is where the human mind turns our survival mechanism into a strategic business plan. This is anger reimagined for personal advantage.

# GETTING OVER

Using anger for profit simply means we must learn to understand that other people's responses to our anger can make us feel powerful and more in control. When this is the case, we may begin using anger to get our way. It becomes strategic, often includes sophisticated plans to make it run, and is goal-oriented. I am defining "anger for profit" as *using anger and angry methods to control the thoughts and behaviors of other people for one's gain.* The word "profit" can be misleading since it is most often applied to financial gain. Profit, as I am using it, simply means that the angry person is using their anger to control other people in a way that it is advantageous to the angry person.

Some of the ways and reasons an angry person uses anger for profit include:

- Showing an angry face before anything happens.
- Being short and abrupt with other people most of the time.
- Being slightly derogatory when interacting with others.
- Being slightly intolerant of other people's positions, routinely.
- Making it known, albeit subtly, that they may react poorly in situations that make them unhappy.
- Making someone wait for a response.
- To practice one-upmanship.
- To control the group agenda or itinerary.
- To be the authority on any given subject.
- To demand payment for deeds done for others.
- To subtly let other people know the desired course of action without stating it directly.

Like its passive-aggressive and righteous counterparts, it is difficult for other people to describe what the angry person is doing when they are using anger to manage them. Most of the time, they are not expressing true anger. They are just introducing the notion of an angry potentiality. Without ever really understanding it, the targets of the anger acquiesce to the will of the angry person, never really comprehending why they are doing so.

The last item on the list is the real objective of a person using anger for profit. They know what they want from the other people, but instead of warmly discussing what they would like to do or, at the very least, suggesting a course of action and waiting for a response, they control the discourse before it becomes a communication item. This reduces the possibility of not getting what they want.

## FOLLOW THE LEADER

A truly gifted leader knows where they want to go and how they want to get there. They want others to follow, but they do not want any dissension among the ranks. They like to push agendas because their plan is important to them, but at other times, it is simply because they enjoy the power that comes from controlling others. People who use anger for profit do so for three reasons:

1. They have difficulty confronting other people honestly and feel that controlling them more efficiently controls the outcome.

2. They are insecure about the possibility of things not going their way.

3. They like the power and control over other people that comes with this type of anger.

You may recall from Chapter 10 that the passive-aggressive user did things to the other person that were hidden from view to address what the other person did without ever overtly addressing it. Anger for-profit uses some of the same hidden mechanisms, but it is not anger that results as a reaction to something someone else did. The target of anger for profit typically does nothing to the person using it. This is *not* a reaction to something someone has done to them, they have not been hurt, and there is no real desire to hurt the other person. This is a form of proactive anger. In this case, the person has decided to use this approach because the possibility of resistance exists, and the anger discourages any possible alternative directions before they are suggested.

People who use anger for profit, in addition to wanting to be the leaders in a situation, do not like to be told what to do and will not entertain the possibility of someone else being the top dog. They are strategic planners, efficient interpersonal diagnosticians, and are tenacious about gaining advantages over other people. While it provides the appearance of power and leadership, being able to control others is an outgrowth of personal insecurities. Anger for profit is a compensatory device where the insecure individual assumes the top position so that they are not challenged and their emotional survival remains intact. Anger for profit is born out of fear and is often tied to past issues of suppression, abuse, and invalidation.

## UNDERCURRENTS; UNCONSCIOUS MOTIVATORS

In Chapter 5, I introduced the notion of undercurrents to anger. To recap, unresolved issues from one's past remain in the unconscious mind and are often motivators for thoughts and behaviors that occur as life continues to unfold. Often, those who use anger for profit become so caught up in the process of manipulating others and the quasi-power that comes from it that they no longer understand the undercurrents in their lives.

It is important to remember that the reason to use anger for power is to not feel weak. Any conscious connection with undercurrents related to past insecurity will create the feeling of weakness and insecurity, and this runs counter to the reason to use anger for profit.

Here are some examples of the undercurrents that instigate anger-for-profit strategies:

- **PERCEIVED INVISIBILITY:** There is the perception that no one sees them as significant people.

- **INTERPERSONAL INVALIDATION:** They feel as though other people do not think that their opinions are valid.

- **REJECTION:** They may feel as though other people have cast them aside and are not concerned about the way they feel.

- **EMOTIONAL ABUSE:** They may have experienced emotional abuse such as insults, criticisms, accusations, and putdowns.

- **PHYSICAL OR SEXUAL ABUSE:** They may have been punched, hit, kicked, or sexually assaulted.

- **FAMILY BREAKUP:** They may have experienced divorce or have been estranged from other family members.

- **UNRESOLVED FEARS:** They may have experienced traumatic events that have created unresolved fear.

- **UNRESOLVED ANGER:** They may be holding on to anger stemming from abuse or victimization from earlier periods in their lives.

- **FEAR:** They fear that others are going to control them, so they make it a priority to control others first.

- **MODELING:** They have witnessed the use of anger for profit by other people in their lives, and they know that it works.

Let's look at an example of a person who has undercurrents of past trauma but does not recognize that his thoughts and emotions have been diverted to using anger for his personal gain:

Adam is a forty-five-year-old mid-management supervisor. He works in the corporate offices of a department store chain and has the responsibility for communicating with other members of the marketing staff. Adam is the newest member of the staff, so some of his responsibilities are mundane, such as making sure others on the team have what they need.

Adam's parents were teenagers when he was born, and he became a ward of the state. He grew up in three different foster homes, and although he was not abused in any fashion, his self-esteem is low. He was moved to three different families and three different school districts before he graduated, so he has difficulty with close relationships and has few friends.

Adam tends to try to direct the flow of meetings even though he does not have all the information or the experience he needs to understand the bigger corporate picture. Rarely smiling or acting in a friendly manner, he can be subtly demanding, often practices one-upmanship, likes to be an authority on most subjects, and can even be derogatory at times. He quietly lets people know how he would like tasks and projects to progress.

Most of the time, what Adam does doesn't bother anyone. At times, however, he has gotten into heated discussions with colleagues who have tried to stop him from asserting his will. This does not sit well with Adam, and he continues to use the same attempts to take control of the meeting.

To counter other members of the team who are attempts to stop him from taking control of the meeting, Adam lets them know he is not happy. He does this by criticizing their plans, the way they operate in the corporate structure, and even by personal attacks. There are time when others either don't understand what he is doing or are just too tired to fight the battle with him. When this happens, Adam is feeling stronger, and as though he has assumed some of the power that he wanted.

This is a simple example of anger for profit. In some cases, the person is more demanding and may not budge when others express their opinions or attempt to change the direction of the event, as we saw with Adam. In other cases, people may resist the efforts of someone using anger for power, and push back. Sometimes, people using anger for profit may back down, but more often, they will either hold their ground or reevaluate their position and return with a redesigned approach. Regardless of the success or failure that comes with using anger for profit, that person will still be seen as an angry person, and someone who tries to use their anger to rise above other people.

# COMPENSATORY POWER

Though I am using the term "for profit," there is no realistic or permanent profit when anger is the guiding force behind this strategy. Earlier, I defined "anger for profit" as *using anger and angry methods to control the thoughts and behaviors of other people for one's own personal gain.* With so many other options available to increase personal profit, why would a person resort to using anger to control other people? A considerable amount of energy is expended simply by maintaining an angry mask. That energy could be more beneficially used if it were applied to more positive and constructive methods. However, the person using anger for profit *is* angry. That is the driving force behind much of what they do.

The conscious focal point may be strategically arriving at a desired goal, but the methodology screams of fear and insecurity. A person whose mind is intelligent enough to strategically use anger to manipulate others and to ensure that they obtain what they want from those people is also intelligent enough to use more positive measures to achieve their goals. Doing so would help them apply their intellectual resources to attain their goal, without expending unnecessary intellectual and emotional resources that include angry and calculated methodologies. Learning that not getting your way can teach you more about getting along with other people, while it creates more personal security in the gains you make when you stop using the mask.

It is, however, important to keep in mind that these are insecure people who have undercurrents of unresolved past issues and who may fear that other people will get over on them. Their insecurity is the real driving force that causes them to use their underhanded methods. So, I will refine my initial definition: *Anger for profit is the use of anger and angry methods to have power over the thoughts of behaviors of other people. This approach is born of insecurity and unresolved life pain or trauma.*

Power cannot coexist with insecurity, and it cannot exist without the resolution of past issues. These circumstances will always interfere with true power. The real definition of "power" is *to be in control of one's body, emotions, and intellect.* True power always comes from the inside. Instead of trying to control other people, it is far more important and beneficial to learn to control yourself. It raises the all-important question, "Do you want to be powerful, or do you want to be happy?"

##  TIME TO TAKE ACTION

1. Take a good look at the undercurrents in your life. Is there past pain or unresolved issues that may lead to present-day insecurity? List any past pain or unresolved issues in some detail. These are important items to share with people you trust, or with a professional counselor.

2. Take an honest look at your communication with others. Are you trying to control what they think or do? If you are, there are other ways to achieve your goals without controlling them. This is also something you can discuss with the counselor.

3. List all the ways you may be trying to control other people or prefacing your interaction with them with anger, thereby causing them to stay on guard in their dealings with you. Be honest.

4. If you have unresolved past issues and feel that you are still in pain or insecure, it is a good idea to make an appointment with a professional counselor. Share your lists with the counselor to help them understand what you are feeling and to plan a course of action to help you. If you choose not to see a professional counselor, at the very least, share your list with people you trust. They might be able to help you be more positive in your approach.

 **DRIVING IT HOME**

Those who use anger often say that doing so allows them to vent and feel empowered. Some talk about it as a motivator and something that provides them with more self-insight. Others say they have more clarity of thought when they are angry, but this probably has more to do with the adrenaline rush it produces, though it is short-lived. And, of course, some use it to hide their insecurities and ensure that their goals and objectives are met. Regardless of any of the temporary benefits associated with anger, its destructive value far outweighs any short-term quasi-positives.

**YOUR DECLARATION IS:** *I will strive to be powerful on the inside and will find my happiness there!*

 **ONWARD**

There is a type of anger that involves lashing out and wanting to hurt the person who hurt you, whether that hurt is real or perceived. The retaliation can be verbal, emotional, or physical. In the next chapter, I examine retaliatory anger, how it develops, and what to do about it.

# CHAPTER 13

# Retaliatory Anger: Reaction with a Plan

*If others attempt to take advantage of you, try not to respond with anger. Stay true to yourself, and never let others influence you to be less capable than you are.*

**PROCESSES TO EMPLOY:** Brutal Honesty, I Over E, Present/Understand/Fix, Slowing Down Life's Pace, Internal Focus, Fact-Finding, Living in the Moment, Settling Past Issues

RETALIATORY ANGER HAS MANY OF THE FEATURES of reactive anger, where you quickly react to someone's words or actions without giving the matter much thought. While the anger itself may strike quickly, retaliatory anger is not expressed immediately. It takes time to be revealed and includes an efficient plan to exact revenge against whoever caused your pain.

Typically, we think of anger as something that fires quickly, but as we have seen in passive-aggressive anger, it can be a bit more sinister, developing as the product of a well-conceived plan of revenge. I define "retaliatory anger" as *a planned vengeful response to something someone does that causes anger or pain.* The keyword here is "vengeful." Revenge is a strong motivator and has the following goals:

- The vengeful act is designed to cause the other person to suffer in some fashion.

- The vengeful act is often more pungent than the original act.
- The vengeful act either evens the playing field or gives its user an advantage.
- The vengeful act addresses the obsessive thoughts that occur after the perceived abuse but before the vengeful resolution.
- The vengeful act helps create boundaries the other person must respect.

"Retaliation" is often defined as *the action of harming someone else because they have harmed you*—or to put it simply, revenge. As we saw with reactive anger, there was an action followed by a quick reaction. In the case of retaliatory anger, however, there is an action followed by thought regarding what to do, and then, finally, the response. Sometimes the response is very well planned, a kind of setup to cause as much pain as possible to the other person.

Retaliatory anger is fueled by energy that is applied to the responsive thought that eventually generates the retaliatory measures. As mentioned previously, that marvelous human brain of ours possesses the ability to receive information via our senses, to think about that information, to plan an efficient response, and to deliver that response. Let's look at the expanded stages of the retaliatory response:

- **STAGE 1**: Receive—In the receive stage, the mind is receiving information. Someone did something, and your brain needs to make sense of it. It compiles the information and processes it, which includes elements of memory, past events, information about the other person, the present environment, and the assessment regarding the danger of an immediate response.

- **STAGE 2**: Thinking—In the thinking stage, the mind takes all the information from the receiving stage and prepares to place it in a format for response. Instead of using a quick emotional reaction, it gathers all the information, prioritizes it, and readies it for the development of a retaliatory plan.

- **STAGE 3**: Planning—The planning stage can also be called the preliminary revenge stage. Here, the mind is planning the assault. It plans where, when, and how the assault will be delivered. It pays special attention to the best way to inflict pain on the other person, makes decisions about any tools or confederates that may be involved in the action, picks the place for the retaliation to take place, and makes sure everything is organized for an efficient retaliatory delivery.

- **STAGE 4**: Delivery—In the delivery stage, the other person feels the pain of revenge. It could be a verbal assault and/or a physical act and may involve witnesses in a social setting. The goal of this stage is to inflict pain, to get even with the other person, and to establish fixed and certain boundaries.

## LEVELING THE PLAYING FIELD

The original assault (that is, what someone did to make you angry) creates an uneven playing field. By this, I mean that the other person has gained an advantage, perhaps causing you to feel weak, subordinate, and/or victimized. No one likes to feel this way. We all like to believe that we measure up to others and that there is equality in the world. When someone does something that embarrasses or humiliates you, inflicts pain, or victimizes you in some other way, you may feel that it is essential to do whatever you can to return to a position of equality.

To level the playing field in a perfect world, you would take the high road. For example, you could reestablish your position of worth by making positive contributions or reinforcing bonds with others. This, however, takes time and doesn't have the potential for immediate gratification that feels so necessary to alleviate the pain that comes from the assault and to quickly restore self-esteem and equality. So, the easiest way to return to an even playing field is to reduce the worth of your opponent.

Reactive anger lets the offender know right away that they have made you angry. The problem with this is that it is letting the other person know that whatever they did to anger you was successful; it validates the intent of their assault. You are in pain, and they are "king of the emotional hill." Because reactive anger is usually emotional and irrational, this type of anger does not even the playing field.

Retaliatory anger, on the other hand, kills two proverbial birds with one stone: You can still get back at the other person but no one witnesses a heated, emotionally charged display of reactive anger on your part. Even though retaliatory anger doesn't exactly present you in your best intellectual light, it does not make you look like an angry emotional reactor.

While revenge has its roots in your emotions, since you have spent time thinking things through, your intellect takes over and the blow you deliver to your adversary now includes the weaponry of a more efficiently functioning intellect. Using retaliatory anger to even to the playing field lets the other person know you are no one to be fooled with. It carries with it the advantage of not losing your cool and reverses positions with the other person. Now it is they who have been victimized, and they must determine how to respond. The playing field has been evened.

## IN THE LONG RUN

Retaliatory anger restores your position in the social order and reduces your feeling of victimization. However, while evening the playing field provides a feeling of satisfaction for a job well done, retaliatory anger is not without its side effects. Using anger changes you. It has its most profound effects when it becomes a routine tool in your life. In Chapter 12, you saw how Adam used anger for profit to routinely get what he wanted; this became part of his identity. The same happens with retaliatory anger, or for that matter, any type of anger you routinely use.

Few people want to be known as an angry person—that is, someone who displays some type of anger often. Those who sporadically get angry and do not hurt others are usually spared that designation since it does not become a way of life. However, it doesn't take long for people who are privy to your retaliatory anger to label you as someone who has no problem causing another person's destruction. Being known as someone who retaliates may help you even the playing field and spare you from future instances of aggression from others, but you must also live with the understanding that others now perceive you as a vengeful person. People tend to shy away from that type of person because they know they may have to pay the price, even for an innocent mistake.

Sometimes, evening the playing field means you are stooping to someone else's level. You retaliate because, in your mind, you feel victimized by someone's words or actions. The old saying that two wrongs don't make a right certainly applies here. Using retaliatory anger may level the playing field, but the field you are now playing on resembles the lowly one used by the person who hurt you. So, when you hurt them back, you are essentially behaving the way they did. If you continue with this strategy, the danger is that this will become who you are. Here is an example to illustrate this point:

> Abby is a twenty-three-year-old graduate student. She is the oldest of three children and comes from a spiritual family. Her father is an architect, and her mother is a registered nurse. Abby is studying engineering and does quite well with her studies. She is an emotionally stable person who usually thinks before she reacts, has many friends, and volunteers at the local food bank.
>
> Abby began dating a fellow graduate student a month ago. She did not realize that another student, Lucy, was romantically interested in this young man. When Lucy found out about the relationship, she said some unkind things to Abby. Soon, Lucy began spreading degrading and cruel rumors about Abby. When Abby left her last class on Wednesday, one of the tires on her car was slashed. The next day, Lucy asked her how her ride home was.
>
> Abby was furious but chose not to react immediately. Instead, she gave the matter some thought and later decided to respond in kind. Abby waited two weeks and then punctured

one of the tires of Lucy's car. This was unusual behavior for Abby, but she felt as though Lucy deserved it. She did not want to continue to be victimized and felt that the playing field was now even. Lucy knew it was Abby who had punctured the tire, but since some time had elapsed between the two tire-damaging events, it was difficult for her to prove that Abby did it. Abby made her point.

While Abby did even the playing field and Lucy got the message not to mess with her, she did so at her own expense. Abby felt conflicted by what she had done, knowing that her spiritual teachings expected her to do things differently. What's more, other people saw her in an unflattering light, including the fellow graduate student she was dating. So, yes, Abby got her revenge, but she also paid the price.

As I have mentioned repeatedly, anger will always be anger. You can't dress it up, you can't hide it, and you can't make it look like something else. It will always be anger. Abby made the right decision to take time to think about what she wanted to do. Unfortunately, her decision used another form of anger to get back at Lucy, and it changed Abby's feelings about herself.

Using anger may provide temporary relief, that immediate gratification that many of us seek when someone does something wrong to us. Unfortunately, those side effects can play a bigger role in changing your life than you might think. The advice here is to delay your reaction as Abby did, but when considering your alternatives, always consider potential collateral damage for any retaliatory deeds and seek more positive ways to address the situation. One usually exists.

**TIME TO TAKE ACTION**

1. Before exacting revenge on someone, consider the price you may pay and the collateral damage to others if you carry out your plan.

2. Consider the four stages of retaliation on page 122. If you are thinking about hurting someone, you can also use those stages to prepare a more positive way to address the situation by infusing them with positive thought, choices, and actions. You can even the playing field without anger.

3. Always remember that immediate gratification usually includes quick emotional responses. You don't have to settle the score right away. In the thinking stage, give yourself the luxury of time to formulate a plan that addresses the issue, helps you set your boundaries, considers collateral damage, and doesn't destroy your feelings about yourself or your reputation.

4. Think about the consequences of any action you are planning to take. Nothing happens in a vacuum. Even if you are putting time between what the other person has done to you and your eventual retaliation, when you act to even the score comma you are taking center stage, and all eyes are upon you. Do you really want to behave like the person who hurt you? Think carefully about this one.

5. When someone does something to you and you are thinking of getting even with them, take time to talk it over with someone you trust who can help point you in the direction of a good decision.

 **DRIVING IT HOME**

The human mind can lift you to higher heights or take you to new lows that will cause problems for you. People will inevitably invade your life with mildly rude to outright horrible behaviors from time to time. These behaviors and actions exacted at your expense can make you feel ashamed and victimized, perhaps compelling you to strike back. Be aware, however, that if you stoop to their level to even the playing field, the price may be your dignity and peace of mind.

**YOUR DECLARATION IS:** *I will think less about revenge and more about taking the high road!*

 **ONWARD**

Using anger often can develop into a routine way of living. The more often something is used, the greater the physical, emotional, and intellectual dependence on it can become. In the next chapter, I discuss how anger can become addictive. I will also help you to keep this from happening, or if it is already the case, help you address it.

CHAPTER 14

# Addictive Anger: Evolving into Dependence

*Anger can become addictive. It reduces you to an emotional mess. Look for peaceful solutions to your problems. They are always there.*

**PROCESSES TO EMPLOY**: Brutal Honesty, I Over E, Present/Understand/Fix, Slowing Down Life's Pace, Internal Focus, Fact-Finding, Living in the Moment, Settling Past Issues, Life Inventory

**IN THE PRECEDING THIRTEEN CHAPTERS, I PROVIDED** of substantial amount of information about anger and the various types of anger one can experience. Each of those chapters outlines how that type of anger develops, manifests, and is expressed. Anger and the subsequent chemical and hormonal changes in the body produce temporary changes that occur during an angry incident. For most people, when the event has ended, the body systems return to normal functioning. What happens when a person uses anger daily and the brain and body need to adjust on a more permanent basis? In this chapter, I discuss how anger can progress to the point that it can produce physical and emotional addiction just like a drug.

The standard definition of "addiction" is a neuropsychological disorder characterized by a persistent and intense urge to use a drug or engage in behaviors that produce natural reward, despite substantial harm and other negative consequences; the fact or condition of being addicted to a particular substance, thing, or activity. Typically, we tend to interpret addiction as applying to a substance. We may reference it in terms of drugs like alcohol, street drugs, or prescription medications. In other instances, we may attach it to conditions like food addictions, sexual addictions, and in today's world, addictions to electronics like smartphones.

Addictions can include continued abuse of any of the following:

- Amphetamines
- Caffeine
- Cocaine
- Exercise
- Food
- Gambling
- Inhalants
- Marijuana
- Opioids
- Pornography
- Sex
- Shopping
- Tobacco
- Video games

## FROM USE TO ABUSE TO ADDICTION

Human addiction usually follows a developmental course in the body. There is a starting point when a person begins to use a substance or involve themselves in a particular activity. As a substance or activity starts being overused, the brain and the other physical systems must accommodate the overactivity. We are back to that habit formation, the brain and body's process of normalizing something that we do even if it can harm us, which I discuss throughout the Fix Yourself Empowerment Series. Again, regardless of whether the activity is healthy or not, the brain and body must accommodate something we choose to continue to do.

As this happens, the brain builds a tolerance to the drug or activity, and it becomes enjoyable, something you want to keep doing. Now, no longer simply an activity or substance, it becomes something the brain is dependent on. When this happens, an addiction is created. For some people, the addiction can be something that, with a little help, you can recover from. For others, it is a much stronger dependence, and the addiction could be a lifelong enterprise.

Once addiction sets in, we lose sight of why we started using it in the first place. Addiction is a physical/neurological condition. You can perform the addictive behavior simply because you are addicted to it, and it alters the way you feel. Anger, just like drugs, alters brain chemistry, and gives you that adrenaline rush you may seek. As a result, you may begin using anger in situations where anger should never apply, such as throwing a temper tantrum because your partner forgot to buy orange juice.

Once your brain chemistry changes, you may introduce situations that can cause you to become angry simply to feel the rush. When you do, you will feel pain relief, believe that you have more confidence, feel as though you have reduced your anxiety, and mistakenly believe that you are more efficient in your daily life. All of this comes from the neurological and adrenaline rush that anger provides, that altered brain chemistry often seen with substance abuse. Make no mistake, anger can behave just like a drug, and the loss of control can be astounding.

Note: The 5th book in The Fix Yourself Empowerment Series, *The Fix Your Addiction Handbook* covers seventeen different addictions, the important information you need to know about them, and what to do with them.

## JUST LOOKING FOR A REASON

Every drug or addictive behavior has its distinct effect on your brain. Some can overstimulate the brain, while others can provide it with a feeling of euphoria. Some will raise the intensity level you feel physically, while others can help you release pent-up energy. In some cases, your anger is a response to something that happened. In other cases, as we saw with anger for profit, passive-aggressive anger, and reactionary anger, there is a mental approach involved.

When anger becomes an addiction—that is, when tolerance is built in your brain and body—your body will look for ways to express anger to receive the adrenaline rush and/or calming effect that accompanies it. Think about someone in your life who seems to look for reasons to be angry. There seems to be an agenda, something they want to happen, and they will pick a fight or do something else to annoy other people to set off an argument. The usual interpretation of this is that the person is just angry and picks a fight because they got angry. The other explanation is that anger has developed into an addiction, and the brain and other physical systems—which are already primed for the episode—are seeking the stimulating and gratifying effects. Here is an example to illustrate this point:

> Al is a thirty-nine-year-old factory worker. He comes from a family where anger was often expressed. He has been known to be short-tempered and abrasive with others. Al is good at his job and well respected there. He has two children, and coaches both of their basketball teams. He has been married to Sheila for twenty-two years. Their marriage has been stable, but Sheila puts up with angry outbursts from Al several times per week.
>
> Today, though everything seemed to be going well, Al's mood changed, and he began to complain about Sheila not getting the laundry done on time. Al has all the clothes he needs and typically only wears jeans and T-shirts. There seemed to be no rational reason for the argument, and regardless of what Sheila did, he would not be satisfied. The more she pressed him to explain why he was angry, the worse things got.
>
> This is not the first time something like this has happened, and it seems like a few times per week Al's mood changes drastically and quickly. There never seems to be any rational reason for his behavioral change. Even when he does have a clear point to make, his anger seems to be over the top regarding what he is expressing his anger about. Aside from his angry outburst, Al treats his wife with respect, is a good father, and is well respected at church and in the community.
>
> When we look at Al's family history, there was constant verbal abuse. Al's use of anger in that environment had more to do with survival than it did with any other type of anger. As he moved into adolescence, the anger became more pronounced, and by the time he was an adult, it was a routine way of behaving. Though he is angry, for the most part, Al does his best to keep from expressing his anger to his wife and children. However, there are times when he feels like he is at the boiling point and reports that when he expresses his anger, he feels

better. He also reports that he's beginning to understand that he is looking for reasons to be angry.

Al began to see a counselor, who diagnosed addictive anger, and they began to chart his weekly cycle. The results show that every three days, Al's anger intensified, and he picked a fight, usually with his wife. As the anger was being expressed, he liked the rush it was providing. After the event ended, he felt better and was much calmer after the episode. Al's counselor has begun to work with Al on his addiction and the angry undercurrent coming from his childhood years that instigates it.

## MILD AND NOT SO MILD

Some people have mild forms of addictive anger, expressing anger once a week or so. This offers a quick fix, provides neurological gratification, and gives their bodies the desired acceleration followed by a calming effect. For others, however, addiction to anger is far more involved. For some, it could be a daily occurrence or something that happens every few days.

Many people experience anger addiction differently, though the fundamentals are usually the same. You find a reason to be angry and your behavior accommodates the angry acceleration. You experience the effect you were looking for and feel the rush that comes from the acceleration. The event runs its course, and soon after it ends, you feel calmer and more relaxed. However, it is important to keep in mind that, for some people, when the event ends, it is also the beginning stages of withdrawal.

Withdrawal is one of the key factors that causes addictive anger to continue to manifest and be expressed. Take the example of a nicotine addict. They smoke a cigarette, and depending on the level of addiction, they will require a cigarette soon after. This could be twenty minutes later, an hour later, or longer. But why do they need to smoke the next cigarette? Many smokers will say it calms them down. This is true, but the reason this calming effect occurs is that their withdrawal has been satisfied, so of course, calm has been restored.

The same is true for addictive anger: The anger is expressed, the person feels the associated acceleration, it relieves some undercurrents that caused the anger to occur, and the person experiences a sense of calm. After some time, however, withdrawal sets in, and the brain and body need to be satisfied again. When this happens, Another angry outburst is needed to produce the same rush experienced during the previous episode.

## ARE YOU ADDICTED TO ANGER?

To determine if you have addictive anger, answer the following questions:

1. Do I feel more confident when I'm angry?
2. Do I like the rush I get when I'm angry?
3. Am I getting angry in situations where anger is not necessary or should not apply?
4. Do I look for reasons to express anger?
5. If I can't find a reason to be angry, do I create one?
6. Do I overreact to situations that simply are not important enough to become angry about?
7. Do I routinely use anger to make myself feel better in some way?
8. Do I feel withdrawal symptoms like agitation, intolerance, and stress when I cannot express my anger?
9. Is it difficult for me to stop being angry on my own?
10. Do I have other addictions or obsessive behaviors in my life?

If you answered yes to most of these questions, anger has probably changed the way your brain is functioning. It is a good idea to see a professional counselor to help you understand why you are using anger, teach you about the addictive process, and help you formulate a plan to address your anger. This will help reduce withdrawal symptoms and assist you in establishing a plan to move forward without this destructive tool taking over your life.

Some people deal with addiction, while others can avoid this life-altering problem. Anything we overuse can create dependence since the reason we overuse it is because it creates euphoria and immediate gratification. Breaking the addictive cycle of anger is not impossible. However, if it has progressed to this point, you may need help. Your task will be identifying the motivators and undercurrents of your anger and settling those issues. It also means learning about addiction, how to stop using anger, and how to remain in recovery.

 **TIME TO TAKE ACTION**

1. Reread and answer the five questions about addictive anger. Be completely honest with yourself. If you answer yes to most of them, you likely are addicted to anger.

2. Chart your behavior for a month to give you an idea of how often you are becoming angry with other people. While you're charting, list how often it happens but also exactly what happened in those situations.

3. Ask someone close to you who sees you frequently to also chart your behavior. You may be surprised to see how often they report your use of anger.

4. Make an appointment with your primary care physician to ensure that no physical concerns are involved in your angry expressions.

5. Make an appointment with a professional counselor to help you through the addictive process and help keep you in recovery from addictive anger.

6. Accepting the idea that anger can become an addiction it may be difficult. Keep in mind that anger changes the way your brain functions. It provides acceleration and the adrenaline

rush that is so prominent with acceleration-based addictions. Be willing to entertain the possibility that your anger may have progressed to the point of an addiction.

 **DRIVING IT HOME**

If you think you are dealing with addictive anger, you are not alone. You do, however, have a choice. You can remain angry and experience everything that goes along with the dependence on it, or you can do something about it. You do not have to remain addicted to anger and the undercurrents that motivate it. You have a choice regarding the way you deal with any situation in your life. Addressing your addictive anger is a huge step in creating a life that is happy, loving, and fulfilled.

**YOUR DECLARATION IS**: *I will address my addictive anger and learn how to live without it!*

 **ONWARD**

Anger is so often turned outward and directed at other people, as we have seen in Chapters 3 through 14 in this book. What happens when anger turns inward and is directed toward oneself? In the next chapter, I examine self-abusive anger, how it develops, and what you can do about it.

CHAPTER 15

# Self-Abusive Anger: Anger Turned Inward

*Turning your anger against yourself is a form of abuse that can destroy every part of you!*

---

**PROCESSES TO EMPLOY:** Brutal Honesty, I Over E, Present/Understand/Fix, Slowing Down Life's Pace, Internal Focus, Fact-Finding, Living in the Moment, Settling Past Issues, Life Inventory, Forgiveness, Trust, Faith, Honor, Dignity

---

IN THE PREVIOUS ELEVEN CHAPTERS, I DISCUSSED the type of anger directed at other people, external events, and objects. In this chapter, I turn the focus to the most insidious form of anger—the type of anger that is turned against oneself. Self-abusive anger is usually associated with shame and negative thoughts. People who experience this type of anger might internalize what they are feeling and take it out in ways that are harmful to themselves, such as drug or alcohol abuse, unhealthy eating (or not eating), or physical harm to themselves.

Self-abusive anger, also called self-injury, self-harm, and self-mutilation, is traditionally defined as *any intentional injury to one's own body*. Usually, self-injury leaves marks on the skin or causes tissue, muscle, and even bone damage. At times, the damage is done quickly, such as cutting or breaking one's finger. The damage can also be chronic and long-lasting without intervention.

To help you understand what causes self-abusive anger, how it manifests, and the damage it causes, I define "self-abusive anger" as *destructive self-harm done to cope with emotional pain and trauma and to provide distraction and relief from abusive circumstances in one's past or current life.* The more common examples of self-abusive anger are:

- **BURNING (OR "BRANDING" WITH HOT OBJECTS):** This can include burns with matches, curling irons, other hot irons, or even the kitchen stove. At times, cigarettes are used and put out on the skin. Burning oneself is a harmful coping mechanism for emotional pain, anger, or frustration. Burning may seem to offer a momentary sense of calm and an emotional release, but it is often followed by feelings of guilt and shame, and permanent scarring. People will often experience the same emotions that triggered their burning episode again. This results in a cycle of behavior that can be difficult to overcome without help.

- **EXCESSIVE BODY PIERCING OR TATTOOING:** Some people say objects piercing their skin bring them relief from emotional pain. Others enjoy having their body pierced with metal and their skin inscribed with permanent ink. Piercing and tattooing, in and of themselves, should not be considered self-abusive anger. It is the enjoyment of the pain involved that qualifies it as self-abusive anger for some people.

- **PICKING AT SKIN OR REOPENING WOUNDS:** Sometimes wounds are accidentally imposed, which is not the problem. However, picking at the site of a wound and/or reopening wounds is done primarily for the associated discomfort. This behavior causes pain, keeps the wound active longer, and distracts those who do it from emotional pain.

- **EATING DISORDERS:** Controlling food intake is often thought of as a way to control one's environment and one's body. These conditions include problems regarding how one thinks about food, weight and shape, and in their eating behaviors. These symptoms can affect one's health, emotions, and ability to function in important areas of life. The more serious cases can evolve into anorexia and bulimia.

- **DEEP SCRATCHING**: Everyone scratches itches. The scratching involved with self-abusive anger is born out of frustration, shame, and guilt. A person typically scratches from situations stemming from their past pain and when the painful and frustrating conditions in their lives do not change. It is also done as another form of branding or because their frustrations build to a point of desperation. It is quite painful, and momentarily distracts the person from the pain, but the shame and guilt soon override any compensatory relief. The scratching usually penetrates several layers of the epidermis, often leaving permanent scars.

- **CUTTING**: Cutting is another way to distract oneself from emotional pain and past traumas. Not unlike the pain that is enjoyed by some people when they receive tattoos, cutting also gives a person a feeling of control and getting over on other people since it is so secretively done. For some, there is a feeling of empowerment. However, consistent with its scratching counterpart, the immediate gains are quickly replaced by the guilt and shame associated with the behavior.

- **HAIR-PULLING**: Hair-pulling (trichotillomania) disorder is often referred to as "trich." It involves the recurrent pulling out of one's own hair despite attempts to stop pulling. It is considered a body-focused repetitive behavior (BFRB) like skin-picking or nail-biting. Initially, it provides relief from emotional pressure. However, it can quickly develop into an obsessive-compulsive behavior.

- **HEAD-BANGING**: We often see this behavior in autistic people, but one does not need to be on the spectrum to perform it. Head-banging is often associated with mental distress, anger, and in more extreme cases, with psychotic experiences, though this occurs in very few people.

- **HITTING (WITH HAMMERS OR OTHER OBJECTS)**: Hitting oneself with hammers and other objects is rare, but it can be another diversionary tactic in which a person is using a more extreme method of pain administration. This usually happens when a person is extremely angry and frustrated and feels as though they have no way out of their emotional pain. While there may be short-term relief, the emotional pain quickly returns.

- **BONE-BREAKING**: This behavior is rare, but it can occur in more serious cases of emotional distress and more often with people who are experiencing deep depression or psychosis. Typically, the person breaks their own fingers and toes. For some, the behavior stems from a reduced ability to feel on an emotional level.

Self-injury generally occurs when people have what seems like overwhelming or distressing feelings. It can also be an act of rebellion and/or rejection of parents' values and a way to individualize oneself. When it comes to self-abusive anger, the keywords are "distraction," "diversion," "control" and "purging."

The act of inflicting pain on oneself, for a brief time, distracts the person from any other past pain or current living situations that are painful or cause distress. The distraction may last for a few minutes, or it may persist for the better part of the day. Where distraction can pull a person away from their pain, diversion directs their attention to something else. Initially, it is the purging of the pain, but it may also be the secrecy of the act, the short-lived sense of empowerment it provides, or any fantasy-like thoughts that may be included during the period of self-harm. For some people, purging is also a temporary release of the guilt and shame that past trauma may have caused or the guilt and shame related to the self-abusive behavior itself.

People who suffer from self-abusive anger often report that their self-injury is a way to:

- Temporarily relieves intense feelings, pressure, or anxiety.
- Distract them from the pain, if even for just a short time.
- Control and manage pain—unlike the pain experienced through physical or sexual abuse or trauma.
- Break through emotional numbness that can be a product of distancing oneself from past pain.

- Ask for help in an indirect way or drawing attention to the need for help.
- Attempt to control others by manipulating them (e.g., try to make them care, feel guilty, or go away).
- Give them something in their life that is personal and completely under their control, as they see it.

## TO CONTROL OR NOT TO CONTROL

Self-abusive anger almost always begins as a strategy to control other people or, at the very least, to gain more control over distressing situations in one's life. This type of anger is also known as non-suicidal self-injury, which simply means the person is typically not trying to end their life. However, in drastic situations, such as if a person cuts too deep, loss of life may occur. There is also a danger that what started as an effort to control oneself, others, and/or situations may progress to compulsive behavior, and the person no longer has control over the self-abusive acts. Self-abusive anger can develop into an addiction.

Over the years, I have counseled many people who suffer from self-abusive anger and who began to injure themselves to escape past trauma and pain and to gain more control over their lives and other people, as they perceived it. When they first started performing the behaviors, they felt the empowerment associated with the act and began to use the behaviors repeatedly to reestablish those feelings. Unfortunately, as their bodies and brains continued to adapt to the self-harm, it became a routine way of life for them, and their physical, emotional, and intellectual tolerance for the behavior increased, which led to repeating the behavior more often and with more intensity.

Since the human body adapts to the pain, the pain from the self-injuring acts needs to increase. Now, cuts and scratches are deeper, hair is pulled harder, and recovery from the injuries takes more time. Like any other addiction, there is a period of euphoria, followed by a period of withdrawal. As the behaviors progress and must become more intense and done more often, addiction continues to increase, and the withdrawal from the self-harm becomes more intense, physically, emotionally, and intellectually.

A behavior that was designed to relieve physical unrest, settle emotions, and give the intellect diversion into a more attractive focal point has devolved into of behavior whose withdrawal wreaks havoc with the body, initiates a period of severe anxiety and depression, and leaves the person intellectually wasted. Consistent with any addiction-based design, even though the withdrawal is imminent after the self-abusive act, the behavior continues. What began as a device of control has become a self-injuring prison with little control.

Once self-abusive anger progresses to the point of addiction, many types of anger, pain, and desperation will make their appearance. Look for reactive anger, volatile anger, reactionary anger, and even passive-aggressive anger. At this point, depression and anxiety become more pronounced and consistent with other forms of addiction, and it becomes difficult for the person to hide what they are doing. This is where people can become desperate, at which point self-abuse and anger can progress to suicidal ideation.

## WARNING SIGNS OF SELF-ABUSIVE ANGER

Signs that an individual may be engaging in self-injury include:

- Wearing pants and long sleeves in warm weather.
- Scars, often in patterns.
- Small patches of missing hair.
- Fresh cuts, scratches, bruises, bite marks, or other wounds.
- Excessive rubbing of an area to create a burn.
- Refusing to change in front of other people.
- Keeping sharp objects close.
- Frequent reports of accidental injury.
- Anxiety and depression.

- Emotional outbursts and impulsive behavior.
- Withdrawing from relationships.
- Expressing feelings of hopelessness or worthlessness.

Seeing these warning signs does not necessarily mean that someone is abusing themselves. However, it does mean that there is a need to investigate the situation a bit more closely. Also, seeing only one of these symptoms does not mean there is a problem. Usually, several behaviors are displayed at the same time. If you are experiencing some of the warning signs listed above, it could mean that you are experiencing abusive anger. It may be time to get help.

## GETTING HELP

In the early stages of self-abusive anger, treatment is not as intense, and the outcome is usually favorable. By the time the behavior has progressed to the point of obsession followed by addiction, there is much more to deal with. If you or someone you know is injuring themselves to cope with emotional distress, past traumas, or even current abuse, the best thing to do is to get help fast.

Self-abusive anger is an extremely difficult form of anger to stop on your own. When anger progresses to the point that you turn it on yourself, you are not only fighting past pain inflicted by other people or situations or even current pain and trauma that may be occurring in your life. You are now fighting yourself, and you may be battling an addiction. Getting professional help is strongly advised. A professional counselor or psychologist skilled in self-harm and addiction can help you address past and present trauma and bring you through the self-abuse cycle and associated addiction.

Anger almost always has those components of insecurity and fear, but self-abusive anger also has a much stronger form of shame and guilt. Often, people who engage in this type of anger have a poor self-image and do not feel they are worthy of any help. Their mind is intelligent enough to understand that not only have they experienced pain from other people but also have become both victims and abusers. There is a tremendous amount of shame and guilt associated with this.

Try to keep this in mind: Self-abusive anger is something you are suffering with. This is not who you are. It is a reaction to serious pain and trauma. You did not know how to deal with it, and you may have stumbled onto a self-harming behavior that initially worked for you. You began doing it, and you lost control of it. It is important to understand that you are still a beautiful person who is worthy of all the good things life has to offer.

Psychologists and professional counselors who deal with this type of anger know exactly what to do with it. This has been a secret you closely guarded for a long time, and they will keep what is happening in the strictest confidence. Take this step and contact a mental health professional who will help you through this. You have nothing to lose and so much to gain.

 **TIME TO TAKE ACTION**

1. If you are hurting yourself and feeling shame for doing so, make the call to a professional counselor right away. Don't waste any time.

2. If, after paying attention to the warning signs of self-abuse, you suspect that one of your family members is hurting themselves, confront the situation and strongly urge them to get help. Do not help them keep their secret.

3. If you feel as though you cannot stop hurting yourself, your abuse may have progressed to the point of addiction. You cannot stop this on your own. Make the call. Let someone help you.

4. If someone close to you has self-abusive behaviors that have progressed to the point of addiction, hiding their blades and other instruments will do nothing. Urge them to get help and support them as they follow through.

 **DRIVING IT HOME**

Self-abusive anger can be a difficult form of anger to recover from. However, many people have recovered—and so can you. The reason this anger is so difficult is that, like addictive anger, it contains an obsessive-compulsive component, and you may not want to stop doing what you think makes you feel good. Regardless of the euphoria involved in self-abusive anger, it is still anger, and it is definitely abusive. Others may have abused you. They did something horrible, but you do not need to continue their legacy. You are worth all the help it takes to come through this. Be willing to get the help. It is time for you to be happy.

**YOUR DECLARATION IS:** *I will let someone in, stop abusing myself, and be the happy person I know I can be!*

 **ONWARD**

All the preceding chapters in this book are designed to give you as much information as possible about anger, the types of anger you may be experiencing, and how that anger affects you and those close to you. What follows in Part Three is the point of the program where I offer you the advice you need to start reducing anger in your life. In the next chapter, I address how you can begin to get your body healthier so that you can keep your anger from destroying it.

# PART THREE

◇◇◇◇◇◇◇◇◇◇

# Building Your Treatment Plan

ANGER IS SOMETHING THAT MANY PEOPLE HAVE, and it is something that, with help, does not have to be a dominant factor in your life. What follows, is your blueprint to help you reduce your anger, and live a happier life.

# CHAPTER 16

# A Healthy Body: Ground Zero

*A healthy body is your first line of defense in the battle to keep anger from destroying you.*

> **PROCESSES TO EMPLOY:** Brutal Honesty, I Over E, Present/Understand/Fix, Slowing Down Life's Pace, Internal Focus, Fact-Finding, Living in the Moment, Settling Past Issues

IN CHAPTER 8, I INTRODUCED THE PHYSICAL effects of anger. I showed you how rapid acceleration affects your skeletal system, muscular system, cardiovascular system, and sensory system. I also discussed deliberate acceleration in which you can have a short interval to decide to engage in the battle. In addition, I discussed how your body is affected just before you become angry, while you are angry, and what happens once the anger subsides. Clearly, there is a significant physical impact. In this chapter, I am going to show you how to keep your body healthy, which can serve three purposes:

1. It can help reduce the physical acceleration before the angry episode begins.
2. It can reduce the physical impact of anger.
3. It can help shorten the duration and intensity of the after-effects of anger when your body is recovering from the shock it received during the angry outburst.

Though triggers for anger, the involvement in the angry episode, and the recovery from anger are often processed intellectually, you are a physical organism first. Your brain, the powerful thinking machine it is, is a physical organ, living in your physical body. Common sense should tell you that your ability to navigate through your environment has much to do with how healthy your body is. Outside of injury, disease, and other chronic conditions, much of the way your body performs is related to how healthy you keep it. The choices you make, healthy or unhealthy, will say much about how efficiently you can address your environment and the quality of your life.

The choices most people make regarding how they keep their bodies healthy often have more to do with their comfort than with what is best for them. For example, challenging oneself physically can be uncomfortable, so someone might do something else such as watch a movie because that falls within their physical comfort zone. There is nothing wrong with engaging in nonphysical activities like going to the movies but not at the expense of activities that enhance one's physical health. Another example is healthy eating choices. Once again, taste tends to take precedence, followed by enjoying that full feeling in one's stomach. The decisions we make about how to keep our body healthy should follow realistic information that is designed for health first and comfort second.

We each have our own routine ways of living our lives, but we will also encounter challenges as our lives unfold. Typically, we keep our bodies healthy enough to deal with a routine day, which may not physically challenge us. As you have learned, anger (especially intense anger) can present significant physical challenges. Even if the angry outbursts is not intense (e.g., using verbal anger as opposed to physical anger), our bodies still experience the physical effects of anger. So, we should keep our bodies healthy, not just to keep up with our daily routines but also to be prepared for challenges we may be presented with, whether they are connected to anger or any other difficulties.

Your goal should be to always keep your body prepared for what you may be presented with, to have the ability to perform efficiently while you are in the middle of that challenge, and to have a short recovery time, both in terms of duration and intensity. Your body is always going to be your first line of defense so it makes sense to keep it strong enough to guide you through whatever life presents you with.

I am not talking about having the ideal body, one that requires long and strenuous visits to the gym, a diet void of anything that you might call comfort foods, or keeping yourself in an overly strict regimen where you are not happy. Your body is a physical machine. It requires that you take the appropriate steps to keep it healthy. Here's an analogy to help make sense of this: Think about the way you take care of your car. If you are taking proper care of it, you are always performing routine maintenance, not abusing it, and promptly addressing any issues that may arise. When you take care of your car properly, for the most part, you can improve the probability of avoiding troublesome breakdowns and expensive repair bills.

## A SIMPLE PLAN FOR A HEALTHY BODY

All too often, people find it difficult to create a viable plan to help ensure their good health. They have a general idea of what to do but do not know where to start. A step-by-step, goal-oriented approach provides an easy and more efficient route to achieve your health goals. As I continue to help you make tasks actionable, I will provide you with a basic road map to get started. Following it can help you create a body that is strong enough to reduce your physical reaction to anger *before it begins*, keep you strong enough during any type of angry outburst, and reduce your recovery time after the angry episode concludes.

Following this simple guide has two benefits that can help make your goal of reducing anger in your life a reality:

1. A healthy body is less susceptible to angry outbursts because the body's ability to relax is increased. This can slow the acceleration process and help you avoid anger and angry outbursts.

2. The intensity and duration of angry outbursts can be reduced since the systems in the body are less affected by any unhealthy physical choices you might think of making.

## Eat a Well-Balanced Diet

The first item on the plan is *eating a well-balanced diet*. A healthy diet, as I define it, provides your daily requirement of nutrients while helping you avoid the wrong foods and any bad habits that can lay waste to your nutritional plan.

Start by keeping it simple, including proteins, vegetables, nuts, and fruits in your diet. This provides you with the proteins, carbohydrates, and fats your body needs. Stay away from large amounts of starches, sugars, saturated fats, and especially trans fats. Portion size is also a concern, so keep your portions on the smaller side, and try not to eat much during the last three hours that precede your bedtime. If you feel you must snack in the evening, a light snack like popcorn without the butter and cheese is advised to avoid weight gain and the potential for gastric reflux.

Feeling full is interpreted in your brain, so eating slower gives your brain enough time to interpret how much food you are ingesting, and it is a great ally in trying to keep your weight down. Also try to stay away from bad habits like gorging, eating in front of the television set, and all those little comfort games you may play with food.

Other culprits that support anger are alcohol, caffeine, energy drinks, and overindulging in the consumption of sugar. Remember, anger accelerates the body, and physically, that is where all the problems start. So, if you are already physically accelerated, expect your anger to be expressed more often and to be more intense as a result. Think about eating for nutrition, not as much for comfort. Feed your hunger, but be healthy about it.

You may notice that I have not attempted to move you in the direction of a specific diet plan. Good eating is sensible eating. Following these simple suggestions will help you eat in a way that is healthy for your body. You can obtain further help by discussing your nutritional needs with your doctor, or you can make an appointment with a nutritionist.

## Get Physical Activity and Exercise

The next item on the list is *physical activity and exercise*. This should be included in your plan as your health and physical ability permit. If you have any physical concerns, check with your physician before you begin any new type of physical activity.

To start your exercise plan, simply try to do any exercise that gets your heart rate up for about twenty minutes daily. This may include either aerobic or anaerobic exercise, swimming, hiking, or even a simple brisk walk around the block. Pick something you think you might enjoy. You can increase the intensity and the duration of your physical activity as time goes on.

It is essential to get your body moving and your heart pumping just a little faster than it does when you are sitting around. You are starting slow, but as your body and brain adjust to your new routine, you will be able to make some incremental adjustments in its intensity.

Think about this: If you eat healthier and exercise just a little more, you are already in a better position than you were before you started. Physical exercise also has the added advantage of releasing stress and anger. Instead of screaming and yelling at someone, run, lift weights, or hit a punching bag. Exercise is a great way to relieve the body of stress and anger.

Exercise keeps your muscles, bones, and all those other systems in your body healthier. As I mentioned in Chapter 8, those are the parts of your body that receive much of the stress on a physical level when you become angry. The goal is always to strengthen your body to keep it healthy and use it as an ally to both prevent you from those angry outbursts and to reduce their duration and intensity.

## Maintain a Proper Weight

Moving on to maintaining proper weight, we already know that part of this is related to a healthy diet. I define "proper weight" as *what is right for you considering your height, bone, and muscle density, and your personal metabolism.* Body charts consider these factors, and while they are not exactly the bible of nutrition, they are great guidelines for where your body weight should be. You can find body mass index calculators online. Use them simply as another guide to help keep you healthy.

Remember, proper weight is not about how you look. It is more about being healthy to optimize your body's resources and the way they can be applied in your daily life. The basic rules for maintaining proper weight are to eat wholesome foods, watch your portion sizes, drink more water, exercise daily, get more sleep, and track what you eat. Like any other process I've talked about, arriving at and maintaining a healthy weight will take time. Make your plan, and then stick with it.

## Get Enough Sleep

The next item is getting enough sleep. Anger and sleep deprivation go hand in hand. You are far more susceptible to angry outbursts when you are tired. When it comes to your sleep, you certainly want to get enough to help keep you healthy. Typically, you want no less than six hours each night. Eight hours of sleep is preferred for most people. The caution here is that people often define how much sleep they need by how much they routinely get. This is not the way you measure how much sleep you need. Remember, your body tries to adjust to the conditions you are presenting it with, but that doesn't mean it is always healthy for you.

Sleep can be one of the most beneficial parts of a healthy life, but it is also one of the more difficult parts of your life to control. Some people fall asleep quickly, sleep through the night uninterrupted, and wake up refreshed. For many others, it is difficult to fall asleep and stay asleep through the night. Work to establish a schedule your body can adjust to. Try to go to bed at the same time every night and wake up at the same time every morning. This routine will help your body adjust to the new schedule. Working night shifts and swing shifts are more difficult to control, but the rule still applies: keep your scheduled bedtime and wakeup times as constant as possible.

Avoid drinking caffeine or alcohol after supper. These substances can cause interrupted sleep patterns even if they don't keep you awake initially. If you need sleep aids, consider natural remedies first, such as supplements like melatonin, hemp oil, CBD (preferably without THC), and herbal teas. Also, avoid violent television shows, video games, or any activity that revs your body up before bedtime.

Make an effort to develop a sleep routine that you can plug into every night. Stay consistent with that routine and avoid making any changes in that plan. This gives your body in your mind enough time to get used to the new schedule. Habit formation takes time, but your body will eventually adjust. Give it the time it needs.

## Restrict Intake of Harmful Substances

The last item is restricting the intake of harmful substances. I mentioned caffeine earlier. Nicotine, for example, weakens your body, especially your cardiovascular system. It can also enhance the possibility of high cholesterol since it helps cholesterol to stick to your veins and arteries. Vaping is another dangerous activity regardless of the active ingredients. The same is true for both street drugs and prescription drugs when used improperly. If you are misusing prescription drugs, contact your physician immediately to help you through this problem. Also, be wary of marijuana use. Regardless of what the proponents say, it is still a drug with side effects.

The simple rule is to put in your body only what was meant to go into your body. Keep it as natural as you can. Avoid continued use of anything that negatively affects you physically, emotionally, and/or intellectually.

Be wary of the long-term effects of any substances you may be using. It is great to enjoy what you are doing but not if it has negative consequences. It's easy to say, "Hey, anything I do will have negative consequences," and then do what causes problems for you. Don't make excuses and use this type of reasoning as a copout. This is your life you're talking about. Making the right decisions is important to help you reduce anger and be happy.

## WHAT ABOUT SUPPLEMENTS?

Although taking supplements is not an item on the simple plan for a healthy body presented here, I advise you to consider the benefits of taking vitamins, minerals, herbs, and other supplements to help your body function properly. A daily multivitamin/mineral is a good place to start. Before you take supplements, however, check with your primary care physician to determine if you need to avoid any particular supplements. Also, if you are taking prescription or over-the-counter medicines, be sure there are no contraindications between these drugs and any add-ons you may be considering.

If you work out regularly and use performance-enhancing supplements or if you use steroids and other body enhancers, be cautioned about the associated dangers. Extended use of these supplements not only causes physical damage, but also plays right into the hands of anger. It is not uncommon to hear reports of people who were experiencing the effects of physical acceleration after their workouts and consequently found themselves in angry confrontations. Steroids are drugs. They are designed to rev your body up, make it bigger and stronger, and give you more endurance. Unfortunately, the nasty side effect is increased anger. Be wary of this one.

## SMALL, CONSISTENT STEPS

You may note that my advice in this chapter is simple and easy to start. It does not get you involved in a complicated process you might abandon quickly due to its complexity. I suggest these little steps to help introduce a healthier way of living into your daily routine and to help you move away from some of the mistakes you may be making that increase the likelihood of anger. These are indeed changes, but certainly ones you can work with. Try not to be overwhelmed, and again, take little but consistent steps.

As you proceed through life, you will continue to be challenged by what other people say and do and anything your environment presents you with. Your body was designed to help you survive the rigors of planet Earth as well as everyone and everything you will experience here. Taking care of your body is always the first step and the most essential ingredient to that healthy and happy life. If you do not take care of your body, it creates the perfect environment for anger to thrive. A healthy body, on the other hand, gives you more control over how you respond to other people and to the events that happen in your life.

A healthy body on its own will not stop you from being angry. That will be a combination of how healthy your body, emotions, and intellect can become. However, it is an important frontline defense that can help you reduce anger's impact on your life and has the added advantage of helping you live a healthier and happier life. You are not attempting to be the healthiest person in the world. You are just trying to be the healthiest person you can be for you.

Give some thought to the advice in this chapter. Ask yourself, "Are there some changes I can make that can help me be healthier in a general sense and help me reduce anger's impact in my life?" You do have control over the way you want to live your life. Think about making healthy decisions. It goes a long way to learning how to reduce your anger and live a happy life.

 **TIME TO TAKE ACTION**

1. Research can be a great friend. Be willing to research what constitutes a healthy body and how you can create yours. Get your advice from the professionals: talk to your physician, listen to health-oriented podcasts, read articles by qualified writers, and visit reputable health-related websites for information.

2. Get enough sleep. If you don't already have one, create a sleep routine and be consistent with bedtime and wake-up time to

ease your body into a healthy sleep schedule. Avoid foods and activities that accelerate your body during the day, especially before you start your pre-sleep routine.

3. A healthy eating plan is essential to a healthy body. There are many reputable online resources and books. If necessary, talk to a nutritionist. Put together an eating plan that helps keep your body healthy, and do your best to stick with it.

4. Alcohol, caffeine, and other drugs and accelerants can exacerbate the possibility of angry outbursts. Do your best to avoid them. If you do consume alcohol, do so in moderation. Remember the rule about putting nothing in your body that does not belong there. Stay as close as you can to the natural course that was designed to keep your body healthy.

5. It is a good idea to schedule a wellness visit with your primary care physician. Be sure to get the necessary bloodwork done to rule out any problems. Ask your doctor about adding a daily multivitamin/mineral or any other supplements such as herbs to your nutritional plan.

##  DRIVING IT HOME

Anger can have severe effects on your physical health. Becoming as healthy as you can is one step you can take to reduce anger's impact on your life. A healthy body is ground zero in your plan to reduce anger's effect on you and those close to you. Getting healthier physically, along with learning to control your emotions and being able to reason through difficult situations is a great way to start your anger-reduction plan, as you will see in the next two chapters. Learn what it means to be healthy, and reaffirm your commitment to keep your body in good shape. Your body will reward you handsomely for the gesture.

**YOUR DECLARATION IS:** *I will keep my body healthy so it can help reduce my anger and live a happy life!*

 **ONWARD**

With anger's effect on the body explained, it's important to understand what role the emotions play both in expressing anger and in continuing to use it in one's life. In the next chapter, I help you understand the role your emotions play in becoming and staying angry. I also provide the information you need to become more emotionally healthy.

CHAPTER 17

# Healthy Emotions: Raising Your Emotional IQ

*Never let anger be your go-to response. Take a step back, think, and respond with a positive plan.*

---

**PROCESSES TO EMPLOY:** Brutal Honesty, I Over E, Present/ Understand/Fix, Slowing Down Life's Pace, Internal Focus, Fact-Finding, Living in the Moment, Settling Past Issues, Life Inventory

---

ACCORDING TO THE AMERICAN PSYCHOLOGICAL ASSOCIATION, the definition of "anger" is *an emotion characterized by antagonism toward someone or something you feel has deliberately done you wrong.* As mentioned in Chapter 2, anger is not purely an emotion. This is a misconception that has led to incomplete methods of treating it. Anger is often classified as an emotion because there is so much emotional expression when it occurs, and it has a profound effect on the way you feel. The goal of this chapter is to help you understand the role your emotions play when you are angry and to help you learn to process anger without your emotions controlling what you do and the outcome of your experience.

Emotions define the way you feel about people and events either as they occur, or as you typically think about them. What's more, your emotions also define the way you feel about yourself. You also internalize feelings about events and circumstances in your life. Because anger is so potent, it can have such a powerful impact on the way you feel that your emotions seem to be overriding every other system in your body. Though you may intellectually process something that makes you angry, if it did not first affect your body and then your emotions, your ability to arrive at a rational solution to whatever is causing your anger would be significantly increased.

*Anger attacks you physically first, and then moves through your emotions, such as fear and annoyance, and finally attacks your mind.* It is hard to recognize this progression because everything is happening so fast. When you become angry, your body and your emotions quickly engage, and you begin to feel it emotionally. You might become more annoyed with someone, or feel your fear level rising. This is why anger is thought of as an emotion. Anger is a physical response that is felt through the part of your brain that processes the way you feel—your emotions. Though it attacks your body first, with its last stop being your intellect, in between those bookends are your emotions.

It can be difficult to understand why anger is primarily a physical response to something when you can feel it so powerfully at the emotional level. As mentioned earlier, emotions emanate from and are felt by your neurological processes, which are lodged in your brain. Your brain is a physical organ. When something happens or someone does something to you, your brain, via your senses, quickly understands that something has occurred; however, that sensation usually lasts for no more than a second or two. As I mentioned in Chapter 5, your brain communicates with all your body systems by using your nervous system to send the appropriate signals to the corresponding systems.

Emotions arise from the activation of specialized neuronal populations in several parts of the cerebral cortex. An anger-provoking situation is initially recognized by your brain. Once again, if you did not physically respond to the anger, your brain would have greater control over the situation. In the case of anger, your body reacts by quickly accelerating. This quick acceleration is what activates the fight or flight response. That acceleration can either cause the anger or make the anger worse. Once your body reacts and you feel the accelerated sensation, this sensation coupled with your mind's understanding of what has occurred triggers your emotions and the angry reaction.

## INTELLECT OVER EMOTION

To reduce anger's impact on your life, you need to learn to be more efficient at controlling your emotions. The process of I Over E (intellect over emotion) is a process I first introduced in *The Fix Yourself Handbook* that revolves around developing the ability to take a step back, put your emotions on hold, and allow your intellect to gather facts. This allows your brain to make decisions based on those facts *before* you have an emotional reaction. It does not suggest that you should suppress your emotions. It simply allows for energy to be directed to your intellectual processing before it goes to your emotions.

Your emotions are a valued life companion, a potent processing ally for your intellect. The I Over E formula is simply a process designed to help you understand the need for intellectual functioning *before* you begin responding emotionally and to give you a practical procedure to reduce your emotional reaction. Since both intellectual and emotional processing are functions of your brain, the formula simply suggests that you put one brain function, your intellect, before your emotions.

The guiding force behind the way your emotions and your intellect operate is very closely tied to your body. The body is the most primal part of our species. Your emotions are more closely tied to your primal instincts than to your intellect. When your body is under assault, it receives energy to fuel the fight-or-flight response. When this happens, your emotions (being more primal) receive some of that energy before your intellectual processes. This influx of nervous energy fuels the emotions, putting the intellectual processes on the back burner. This is important to execute the primary fight-or-flight response in the early moments of a threat, or a perceived threat. Attempting to think about what is occurring during this brief survival reaction could put you in danger.

As you are feeling the physical effects of anger, your emotions and your intellect can take on entirely new identities. On the turn of a dime, what was clear and concise becomes confused and conflicted. What was calm and tranquil has become disorganized and chaotic. It feels as though your mind and emotions have traded places.

Information that is necessary for your brain to function efficiently has been diverted to your emotions, and they seem to be insanely running your out-of-control life show. The combination of physical acceleration, and this energy diversion is what is responsible for angry outbursts and making decisions that are not always in your best interest. Your brain has not begun to receive the energy it needs to function efficiently.

Energy distribution is a key factor in your brain's ability to execute all the tasks it is charged with. These include intellectual pursuits and the regulation of your body's complex life-giving and sustaining processes. Emotions can introduce conflict and confusion into that marvelous brain of yours, and suddenly, your world has devolved into a chaotic mess. So, the I Over E process suggests nothing more than helping you learn to reverse the energy trade that was made, allowing your intellect to receive the appropriate amount of energy first. This helps you reduce the rapid impact of your emotions and assists you in making healthier, more practical choices regarding what to do when you become angry.

To help you understand how anger moves into your emotions during an angry episode, here is an example:

> Eddie is a thirty-seven-year-old physician's assistant. He works in a private practice with a group of internal medicine doctors. Eddie is active in sports, works out regularly, and enjoys spending time with his dog, Samson. Eddie is an even-tempered person, but he can be excitable and, at times, is a quick reactor.
>
> Last week, in a game for the basketball league he plays in, he got into a small altercation with another player, Joe, over what he felt was a flagrant foul. They argued for a minute or so and then let the matter go. Though nothing serious was made of the situation, neither Eddie nor Joe forgot what happened, and both left with some animosity toward the other. Nothing happened during the next two games, but it was evident to Eddie's coach that something was wrong because Eddie seemed distracted. He cautioned Eddie to control his emotions.

As the regular season wound down, both teams qualified for the playoffs. There were sixteen teams in the playoffs, and both Eddie's and Joe's team made it to the final four. As fate would have it, they would be playing each other for the right to advance to the championship game. Eddie still felt animosity toward Joe but decided he would not start anything. However, he also affirmed to himself that if Joe challenged him, he would not back down.

The game was on a Friday evening, with the championship game scheduled for Sunday. Both players were suited for the game, and the first half was a closely fought battle but uneventful.

Joe knew that although Eddie wouldn't start anything with him directly, Eddie would react if provoked, as he tended to do. Joe decided to use this to his advantage to "get in Eddie's head" in the second half.

A few minutes into the second half, Joe bumped into Eddie a couple of times. It wasn't a foul situation, but Eddie knew what Joe was doing. When it happened again, Eddie had a few words for Joe, but nothing escalated between them. Then, as Eddie's teammate passed the ball to him, Joe finally committed one of his patented flagrant falls, and Eddie fell to the floor and landed on his non-shooting elbow. The foul was called, but Eddie was now primed and ready to go. Eddie's anger was rising, he was responding verbally, and everyone could see it beginning to happen.

From Eddie's perspective, he knew Joe was behaving badly to get a reaction from him. So Eddie's brain already understood what was happening. Eddie could feel his body tightening and the anxious feeling in his stomach was beginning (muscular system). His heart was beginning to pound harder and faster (cardiovascular system). He was watching everything Joe was doing (sensory system), and his posture was changing (skeletal system). Eddie was getting angry.

It is interesting to note that before Eddie's body began to feel the effects of the anger, he wasn't doing anything to retaliate. Even when the foul occurred and Eddie hit the deck hard, he was still in control of his actions. However, when Eddie's body began to react, he became furious. He could feel the anger in every part of his body, but more importantly, he could not get his emotions under control.

Initially, Eddie's brain understood Joe's underhanded intentions, but he was still in control and able to keep from reacting. As his anger moved from his body into his emotions, the energy that was fueling his brain was now being fed to his body and his emotions. Logic seemed to have abandoned Eddie, and he was fixated on revenge. The next time he got the ball, Joe attempted to guard him, and Eddie quickly brought his elbow around the front of his body and slammed it into Joe's face.

Eddie received a technical foul and a warning that he would be ejected from the game if it happened again. Eddie's coach pulled him from the court and instructed him to sit and calm himself. Eddie was no longer involved in the game, but he was still angry, his heart was still racing, and he still felt tightness all over his body. It took about ten minutes for the physical effects to subside, and he convinced his coach to let him return to the game. When Eddie got back on the court, his body was a bit more relaxed. He felt less emotional, and his brain was able to think more logically. He was able to think more efficiently and no longer reacted to what Joe was doing.

So, what happened during the game and, more important, during those ten minutes that Eddie sat on the bench? Those ten minutes gave Eddie's intellect enough time to regain its place over his emotions. During the game, Eddie's emotions controlled what he did (E Over I instead of the reverse). If his intellect had been receiving enough conscious energy, it would have helped Eddie make decisions to benefit his team rather than get even with Joe. However, as Eddie's body tightened, his body accelerated, and the acceleration quickly resulted in an emotional reaction. There, Eddie was no longer in full control of what he was doing, resulting in his temporary removal from the game.

During Eddie's ten-minute hiatus, he had a decision to make. He could angrily storm off the court and leave the facility, he could march back onto the court and settle the score with his opponent, or he could give his mind the option of reviewing the situation. When he did that, he redirected his energy to his intellect and reviewed the facts that were important to make the proper decision, which he eventually made. This is an example of intellect over emotion (I Over E). If Eddie understood how to direct more energy to his rational thought processes *before* the incident developed into a potential crisis, he could have made a more intelligent decision before the event escalated. In this example, he might have talked to his coach or clued the referees into what was happening so the focus could have been on Joe.

## POWERING DOWN: 8 PRACTICAL STEPS TO REDUCE THE INTENSITY OF YOUR EMOTIONS

I cannot stress enough how important it is to try to calm down and put your intellect before your emotions. Here are some practical steps you can take to help you start the process:

1. Hit your pause button. If you can, stop for a moment to give yourself some time to decide what to do next.

2. If you can't pause, try to remove yourself from the situation. Stepping away from whatever is going on gives you time to review the facts.

3. Emotions can cause your body to accelerate. Take slow, deliberate, deep breaths to help your body decelerate.

4. Since your body is tightening during acceleration, doing some physical stretching helps relieve the muscle tightness that has developed.

5. Use visualization. Try to visualize yourself calmer to help remove your attention from the emotions you are feeling.

6. Talk to someone who might be available. Ask them to help you calm down, and review the facts with them.

7. This may be the most important step: Make a conscious decision to stop, think, and respond. Say the words "I stop. I think. I respond." Take a few deep breaths, review what you know to be true about the situation, and decide how to respond without using your emotions, and with sound intellectual reasoning.

8. Practice putting your emotions aside and making sound intellectual decisions based on the facts in situations when you are not angry. This will help you make the transition from a reactor to a thinker. Your brain will learn to adjust to this new life skill and it will be easier for you to transition From emotional to intellectual in episodes were anger may be involved.

Reducing the intensity of your emotions and learning to express your intellect first are difficult behaviors to adopt. However, if you keep working on taking these seven practical steps and applying them in your life as often as you can, you will see changes, albeit small ones. You can apply these important steps in your life anytime you are faced with a choice of how to respond. If you can slow down for a moment, review the information, and make decisions based on information in routine situations, you are more likely to use this tool in anger-provoking times. Taking these steps routinely trains your brain to become more efficient and to make better decisions in times of crisis and pressure. Permanent change begins there.

## THE REALISTIC PERSPECTIVE

While emotions play a vital role in survival, happiness, and productivity, like anything in our lives, they need to be expressed in a healthy fashion. What does it mean to express emotions in a healthy way? I will start answering that question with my definition of "healthy emotions." *Healthy emotions are the product of balanced energy distribution in the brain. They are expressed when facts have been intellectually gathered and arranged in a cohesive and big-picture presentation.*

This means that you do *not* want to express your emotions quickly. You want to be able to let them have their say based on factual and intelligent information. You want to provide your brain sufficient time to gather the facts before you start to express your feelings about them. If you react to something before your brain has had adequate time to interpret the information, you risk making a quick decision without the necessary facts. Decisions made emotionally tend to be problematic, since important information may have been passed over initially. So, how does this relate to anger?

Anger can move fast. When you move fast, you emote before you think or, at the very best, while you are trying to think. This interferes with your brain's ability to gather the information you need to gain a clear understanding of what is happening and to resolve any problems you may be experiencing. I preach the notion of intellect over emotion (I Over E) because healthy emotions are always based on life situations that can be placed in perspective. When your perspective is realistic, you can emotionally respond to something that is a clearer and more accurate representation of what is happening in real time. When you do, you are raising your emotional IQ.

When you are angry, your body is going fast, and you are, at the very least, more uncomfortable due to this accelerated pace. Your brain feels as though it is becoming scrambled, and you cannot seem to get a clear picture of what is going on. You can feel as though you are out of control, overreacting to emotionally provoking situations, and losing some of the intellectual control you need to make good life decisions. Understanding how to begin the process of decelerating your body will give your brain enough time to begin its role of interpreting information efficiently for you. Remember this: the way you begin to react in the first few seconds in any situation sets the stage for how you will respond as the situation unfolds. It doesn't have to be that your intellect is more important than emotions, but you do need to use your intellect *before* your emotions.

Before you allow your emotions to impact the information being presented—that is, before you react to an anger-provoking situation—it is important to learn how to hold on to those emotions, at least until your brain can gain an accurate understanding of the facts. This not only keeps you more rational and helps you avoid the pain you may cause others and yourself, but also puts you in a position to make the good decisions that are necessary to keep you happy and healthy.

If you are overreacting to what is happening, you can lose sight of the information you need to efficiently address the situation. This isn't to say that you cannot be emotional or that you cannot express your emotions. It simply says that you want to give your brain enough time to present and interpret the facts before your emotions take over. You just want to have the correct information before you make important decisions that may have a significant impact on yourself and others—and potentially alter the course of your life.

##  Time to Take Action

1. Go slow. Few facts are accurately registered in the brain while it is under pressure. Slow down and allow yourself enough time to gather the facts, exactly as they exist. Start by slowing down your breathing.

2. Make a conscious decision not to react quickly. Say this to yourself: "I am not going to react until I give myself enough time to think things through".

3. Begin working with the "8 Practical Steps to Reduce the Intensity of Your Emotions." Try to include them in your daily routine.

4. At times, you will become emotional before you give yourself enough time to think. When this happens, slow down a bit, and remove yourself from the situation. Take a walk or anything that can distract you from your emotions. Return once you feel less emotional and have had the opportunity to review the facts.

5. Your emotions will ultimately enter any situation you are involved in but ideally after you organize the facts. There is nothing wrong with having feelings about a situation, but try to make sure your feelings align with the facts first.

6. If you have difficulty slowing down and removing your emotions from the situation, ask someone for help. Make an appointment with your primary care physician to ensure that a physical problem is not impeding your process. An appointment with a professional counselor may help, too.

 **DRIVING IT HOME**

As soon as something triggers anger, your body accelerates, and your emotions quickly begin to exert their influence. Typically, your intellect receives more energy than your emotions. However, when you become angry, the energy allotment shifts to favor your emotions. In fact, they receive significantly more energy at an accelerated pace. This is the fuel that makes anger work. It is so important to learn to keep the distribution weighted in the direction of your intellect. Work with the "8 Practical Steps to Reduce the Intensity of Your Emotions" to allow your brain the time it needs to gather the facts before your anger causes pain, loss, and repair time which you simply do not need in your life.

**YOUR DECLARATION IS:** *My intellect comes first; my emotions can have their say later!*

## ONWARD

Anger is often a conscious mechanism. We can plan to use it to try to achieve a desired outcome, or, at a minimum, we are aware of our anger as we express it. In the next chapter, I delve deeper into the cognitive component. The focus is on how your brain receives information when you are angry. I also discuss how to use your mind to rise above this angry antagonist.

CHAPTER 18

# Healthy Mind: Empowering Your Thinking Machine

*A healthy mind is a single-minded warrior in the fight against the ravaging effects of anger.*

---

**PROCESSES TO EMPLOY:** Brutal Honesty, I Over E, Present/ Understand/Fix, Slowing Down Life's Pace, Internal Focus, Fact-Finding, Living in the Moment, Settling Past Issues, Life Inventory

---

**AS YOU KNOW, YOUR BRAIN IS AN INFORMATION-PROCESSING MACHINE.** It works in milliseconds, controls memory, rational thought, fact-finding, and decision-making, and is involved in one way or another with the performance of every body system. Regarding the more autonomic systems that regulate involuntary physiologic processes including heart rate, blood pressure, respiration, digestion, and sexual arousal, the brain does not apply as much conscious thought to help make them run. However, when it comes to conscious thought, fact-finding, information-gathering, and intelligent decision-making, conscious energy is required.

Being able to consciously focus on something happens when your mind has enough time to initiate the processes that lead to efficient neurological functioning. Efficient neurological functioning, as I define it, is *the ability of the brain to understand what is happening environmentally and to organize information to help you effectively devise and carry out plans to address any situation that may arise.* When your body is not experiencing anger-based acceleration and your emotions are not overriding the intellect, your brain's ability to interpret information and act upon it can happen without distraction or confusion. However, when energy is being diverted as a result of an overstimulated body and overreactive emotions, its efficiency can be severely compromised. To help you understand how this happens, let's look at some of the simple science that explains what happens in your brain when you are angry.

Anger increases your systolic blood pressure (the pressure in your arteries when your heart beats). When you get angry and physical acceleration occurs your systolic blood pressure increases, which creates the rapid, pounding heartbeat that often accompanies angry outbursts. When your systolic blood pressure rises and your heart begins to pound, the rest of the body systems feel the pressure and join in, preparing you to respond. So, what's happening to your brain when all these changes are taking place? At the risk of being just a bit scientific, this is what happens when your brain is subjected to anger and angry outbursts.

## YOUR ANGRY BRAIN

Two areas where the emotional brain can overfire when you become angry are the insula and the amygdala. The insula creates a brain map of how our body feels during situations. The amygdala encodes the quality, such as positive or negative feelings, and the intensity of your emotional reactions. The degree of activity in the amygdala and the insula is partly controlled by two areas of the thinking brain: the orbitofrontal cortex and the ventromedial prefrontal cortex. When these areas of the brain are operating efficiently, you can think about what you are going to do before you make a potentially problematic decision. Also, your ability to empathize with others is controlled in these two areas of the brain.

When your brain is operating efficiently—that is, when it is not under stress, experiencing excessive fear or pain, or in the throes of an angry outburst—these areas of the brain can operate normally. Thoughts are organized, realistic, and rational, and the brain is better able to understand the bigger picture in any situation as it pertains to you and other people. So, what does anger do to your brain?

In both *The Fix Your Anxiety Handbook* and *The Fix Your Depression Handbook*, I discuss how neurotransmitters work in the brain, how they stimulate the brain to efficiently think and act, and what happens when the brain is deprived of balanced neurotransmitter production. An important point to understand about anger is that it alters the way your brain perceives information. Being primarily a physical condition, anger alters the way your body produces neurotransmitters and other hormones, all of which are extremely important to keep your brain functioning normally. These chemicals do everything from keeping you calm and relaxed to helping you think clearly to organize information and make sound decisions, and to running or helping to run every system in your body.

The important question is, what happens to these neurotransmitters when we begin to feel angry and when a full-blown angry episode commences? Anytime something changes in the way your body works, especially something as potent as anger, the function of your brain is altered in response to that change. Your neurotransmitters and other hormones play an essential role in these changes. They help your brain understand what is occurring and organize the information that will be used to address the situation. This happens all day long as you move from one situation to another. It is a typical everyday process that constantly has your brain adjusting and efficiently dealing with the people, places, and things you are experiencing.

When your neurotransmitters are functioning properly, your brain makes these changes without you even realizing it. At times, when situations are a bit more challenging, the changes can still be made, and you may still be cognizant of what is happening around you. For example, if your hour-long ride to work each morning takes you along the same route, any minor changes like a little more traffic or altered weather conditions can be handled by your brain without you realizing that any chemical changes occurred. However, if you are involved in a minor accident, your body and your emotions may accelerate, and your brain has a little more work to do to get you through it. In this case, you will be just a little more aware of the stress your brain is experiencing.

As neurotransmitter production is either increased or reduced or produced in a state of imbalance, the signals your brain receives and subsequently sends to the rest of your body through its complex neurological pathways can become compromised. The theory is that a deficiency in the neurotransmitter norepinephrine occurs in the brain. Other neurotransmitters like dopamine, serotonin, acetylcholine, histamine, and norepinephrine are necessary for the brain to operate normally. When you become angry, neurotransmitter production is changed, and your body responds. This is part of the physical changes that occur to accommodate the fight or flight response. Remember that response is designed to deal with immediate threats or perceived threats and to help you react quickly. Unfortunately, this altered neurotransmitter production doesn't work well for your brain as it applies to fact-finding and making sound intellectual decisions. Since these chemicals have much to do with mood and physical tranquility, when there is an imbalance, the setting for anger to be felt and expressed has been established.

So, there are chemical changes in the brain, and during periods of anger. The more intense changes are realized with the rapid and extreme types of anger, but there are also subtle changes in the more deliberate forms of anger like passive-aggressive anger. The reason for this is that these chemicals, having their effect on the normal processes of your brain, are compromised. Since tranquility and mood have been compromised, there are increases in obsessive thinking, which as we know, perpetuates deliberate forms of anger like passive-aggressive anger and even retaliatory anger.

### Your Angry Brain Activated

Consider this brief example to make all this brain stuff just a little more functional. It's a typical day for you. You are out with some friends and decide to take a walk in the local park. Everything is going well. You are feeling relaxed, and you are enjoying yourself. One of your friends who has a reputation for teasing and poking at people turns his attention to you. He is not particularly nice as he is criticizing the way you dressed that evening.

You have a history with this person, and at times it has gotten intense and even a bit physical. There has been some pushing back and forth in the past. He is relentless this evening, and now while he is criticizing the way you dress, he's tugging at your jacket. You gave him a warning, but that only makes him more tenacious about getting you to react. He attempts to tug at your jacket again, and you grab his hand. You can feel your heart beating faster, you are no longer relaxed and happy, and your muscles are tightening. Your attention narrows and becomes locked onto the target of your anger. Soon you can pay attention to nothing else. In quick succession, additional brain neurotransmitters and hormones (among them adrenaline and noradrenaline) are released, which trigger a lasting state of arousal. You are not backing down, and you are ready to fight.

If you are following the sequence of action, you may note that this is exactly what I have been talking about in the last two chapters. Your brain already knew that something was going on, and you may have even taken some initial steps to stop things from progressing. When the other person does not cooperate, your physical symptoms begin. Now, instead of reasoning your way through the situation, your attention narrowed, and you became locked into a more drastic way to deal with your adversary. Your brain did initially attempt to take some steps to address the problem. When that did not work and anger began, it started with your body, moved into your emotions, and finally a full-blown angry episode was unleashed. Neurotransmitter production changed, and so did the way your brain dealt with the situation.

Very rarely does anyone's anger simply explode. It usually follows the foregoing progression. Initially, your brain will understand that there is a problem. Its first step may be to attempt to mediate the situation. That could take a few minutes or it may only last a few seconds, depending on the situation. When the initial attempt at mediation fails, your body feels the acceleration, it works its way into your emotions, and before you know it, your rational thought processes are reduced. You are angry.

Once again, even though it may look like a switch suddenly gets flipped, some type of progression is usually involved. Referring to those undercurrents mentioned earlier, they are typically memories of traumatic or painful experiences. At times, resentment and revenge can trigger an angry episode. Even if there is no immediate trigger, those undercurrents are lodged in your brain, so, for some people, the brain is already predisposed to become angry quickly.

Almost everyone has undercurrents. They are those little memories that kind of poke us every now and then. For the most part, they do not cause us any problems, and we can often learn from them. Some of those memories, however, are more emotionally charged. Remember, your cognitive processes and your emotions both reside in your brain. Something interesting can happen when a person or external event begins to make you angry. Not only are you angry about what is occurring, but those emotions can quickly attach to past events, and the intensity and duration of your angry episode may increase.

I have discussed how anger progresses through your body, into your emotions like fear and annoyance, and finally settles in your intellect. Your brain has its own progression through anger. If you go back to the example, the first thing you try to do when the other person tugs at your jacket is to mediate—that is, to do something to quickly stop the problem. So, in that example, your brain starts by attempting to cognitively address the situation. If we keep the matter simple, we can just say that that attempt did not work, and you got emotional, but there is more involved.

Sometimes the choice you make is the product of enough thought to arrive at an efficient solution. Other times, like when you are angry, your brain must accommodate and provide you with additional angry resources to fend off the threat. So now, while your body is tense and reactive and your emotions are hell-bent on destroying the opposition, your brain is trying to figure out a way to make it all happen. If you have chosen to stay and fight, the only goal your brain has is for you to be successful, fend off the enemy, and survive. So, if you're following along, your body and your emotions set the stage for the angry episode to commence, but your brain, understanding that the battle is going to begin, prepares to join the skirmish.

## COMING FULL CIRCLE

In Chapter 8, I talked about homeostasis, and the balance that is so necessary to live happy, healthy, and productively. Your brain never stops trying to move you into a position of balance. So even as it is bringing you through the angry episode, its big-picture goal is to bring balance back into your life. That is what happens after the angry episode and you go into that period of exhaustion followed by relaxation, followed by retroactive thinking. Now, your brain is trying to fix the situation and help you feel good again.

Once anger subsides, levels of neurotransmitters like norepinephrine return to normal levels, and your thinking brain is reactivated. Your ability to empathize returns, possibly causing remorse and guilt over the damage your anger may have done, and you may wish to repair it. The amount of time it takes your brain to return to normal functioning has much to do with how long you were angry, how intense the angry episode was, and how often in your life you become angry. Once again, your brain will adjust to the way you are telling it to live. If you tell it to be angry often, it will attempt to accommodate. If, on the other hand, anger is not something that is part of your life, your brain will function accordingly. The more we use our thinking brain to evaluate our behaviors, including how they might affect the course of our lives and others, the more balance we can infuse into our decision-making processes.

## 7 WAYS TO HELP YOUR BRAIN OVERCOME ANGER

1. Avoid negative thinking and negative internal language. Notice it and then make a conscious choice to redirect your thoughts.

2. Settle past issues that may be undercurrents to anger today. Let people you trust help you with this.

3. Try to give yourself at least five seconds before you respond to an angry trigger. If you must, count to five in your head. Keep in mind though, that this is not a countdown that leads to your angry outburst. It is a five-second pause to help your brain make a constructive decision.

4. Remove caffeine diet pills, energy drinks, and other stimulants from your daily diet. At the very least, cut down on them.

5. Practice breathing exercises throughout your day.

6. Include self-calming techniques such as meditation, yoga, and prayer in your daily life. Practice then for about five minutes several times per day.

7. Share what is in your mind with someone you trust routinely, such as a close friend, family member, or a professional counselor.

    This magnificent thinking machine that guides our lives can adjust to almost anything we present it with. It is our choice regarding what kind of energy we choose to provide our thinking machine with. For some people, a neurotransmitter imbalance causes the problem. For others, it may be more about the choices they make or the undercurrents that may trigger angry outbursts.

    Your brain can have much to say about how anger is expressed and, for that matter if it is at all. So, be diligent about taking care of your brain. If you are having difficulty with anger and your thinking machine either remains angry or is prone to angry outbursts, be willing to get help. Your intellectual brain lies in your physical body, so get things started by making an appointment with your primary care physician. If necessary, talk to someone, a family member, a friend, or a professional counselor. Give your yourself the opportunity to move past your anger into a healthier way to think and, subsequently, to live.

## ⏱ Time to Take Action

1. Since your brain often reacts to angry thoughts and language with angry outbursts, it is important to understand how this is affecting you. Make a list of any recurring angry thoughts or internal language you have. You can talk about your list with someone you trust or a professional counselor, if necessary.

2. Anger is often the result of an accelerated body. Try to remove the accelerants from your daily diet.

3. Practice deceleration techniques like breathing, yoga, prayer, and meditation daily.

4. Practice rational thinking during the day. In any situation that enters your life when you are not angry, discuss the logical choices that can apply there. Doing this will help your brain think logically and practically, and this helps you during those times when you may start becoming angry and need to make good decisions.

5. Try to incorporate the "7 Ways to Help Your Brain Overcome Anger" in your daily life.

6. Learning to reduce the impact of anger in your life requires doing things differently. Learning occurs with repetition over time, and this can best be served by talking to someone who can help you put past events into a coherent perspective and teach you alternate ways of thinking and behaving that you can learn and repeat daily. Be communicative with those you trust about what you are thinking and experiencing. This helps you begin to slow the emotional response to anger, keep your neurotransmitters in balance, and gives your brain the ability to use its thinking powers to help you avoid those anger responses.

 **DRIVING IT HOME**

The human brain is a complicated and adaptive organ. It tries to accommodate the decisions we make, even when they may not be in our best interest. Anger changes brain chemistry, and that has much to do with how we process and act in angry situations. Though anger may work its way through your body, followed by your emotions, and finally your brain, your brain can have much to say about how you learn to reduce your anger. Give your brain an opportunity to understand what anger-free living is about, and it will return the favor by giving you the resources to help you create a new way of living.

**YOUR DECLARATION IS**: *I will do what it takes to train my brain to learn how to be reduce my anger and live a happier life!*

 **ONWARD**

While you are learning to become less reliant on anger, it is important to include some coping strategies and other temporary measures to help you deal with anger. In the next chapter, I discuss some short-term defensive strategies and coping skills, and how you can incorporate them into your life.

# CHAPTER 19

# Coping Devices: Short-Term Defensive Strategies

*Anger can have a devastating effect on your world. Have a plan to divert its negative energy before it takes control of your life.*

---

**PROCESSES TO EMPLOY:** Brutal Honesty, I Over E, Present/Understand/Fix, Slowing Down Life's Pace, Internal Focus, Fact-Finding, Boundary Setting, Living in the Moment, Settling Past Issues, Life Inventory

---

IN A PERFECT WORLD, YOU WOULD NOT have to live with anger, and you would not have to put up with people who make you angry. Almost everyone talks about what it would be like to live in a world where everyone loved one another, was helpful and cooperative, and always worked for the common good. Unfortunately, that is not the way the real world works. We live in an imperfect world with other people from all different walks of life. Sometimes we get along well but other times not so much.

You may be working diligently to reduce anger in your life, but this does not mean that the rest of the world is on the same page. Not everyone understands their anger, and not everyone admits they are angry. Even though you may have come to terms with your need to reduce anger in your life, not everyone else has. Expect other people and events in this imperfect world to continue to poke at you and get you angry. In this chapter, I am going to teach you some strategies to deal with these people and events. I will also explain what coping devices are and how you can use them in your imperfect world.

## MIDDLE GROUND: STAYING THE COURSE

Somewhere in the middle of your fight-or-flight response lies an area where you can't always beat someone up or run from them. Neither strategy seems to be the optimal way to deal with the situation. For example, you may be in a long-term relationship and your significant other has that annoying tendency of doing things that make you angry. You have tried to talk to them about it but to no avail. They don't seem to care, and they continue to do those things that rub you the wrong way and have you on the brink of "ringing their neck."

You certainly don't want to give in or enable their ridiculous behaviors, or leave the relationship, and it doesn't make a lot of sense to do physical damage. So, fight and flight aren't exactly rectifying the situation. You are going to stay with them, and somehow, you must survive their insolent, childish behaviors. So, this is where you call on your thinking machine to become your strategy machine. This is where you activate that territory that lies between hurting them and leaving them. This is where you learn to use coping skills. What follows is a list of coping strategies you can use in anger-provoking situations or when someone is doing something that can trigger your anger. Some of them are important to use as anger is developing or if you are in the throes of an angry episode. Some of the others can be incorporated into your daily routine to help you learn to be more relaxed routinely.

**IMAGINE A CALM PLACE**: A calm place is often used in programs like systematic desensitization. It includes thinking about a special place that helps you feel calm like the beach or the mountains. Imagining this place for a few moments can give you a short break from your angry feelings. In some cases, if you can remove yourself from the situation, imagining a calm place can last for several minutes or longer. This coping strategy helps take your mind away from the angry moment and replaces it with something that makes your brain, emotions, and body feel calmer.

**USE A BREATHING-DECELERATION PROGRAM REGULARLY**: Slowing your breathing down can go a long way in helping you to become a calmer person. Do breathing exercises as often as you can each day. They only take a minute or two, and you can do them almost anywhere. You can find instructions for various types of breathing exercises from reputable sources online.

**DO INTERNAL SENSORY EXERCISES**: Grounding is a self-soothing technique. It's usually applied in times of stress, which can happen when you become angry. Examples include using soothing objects like spinners and rubber bands or cognitive games like identifying colors. More efficient sensory exercises consist of identifying pleasant objects or people in your immediate environment and directing your attention to them.

**EXERCISE REGULARLY**: As discussed, much of the anger you feel can be physical, so exercise is a great way to relieve the energy that can drive angry thoughts and episodes. Start exercising regularly, but first, schedule an appointment with your primary care physician to make sure you are healthy enough to do so.

**PRACTICE RELAXATION TECHNIQUES**: There are many relaxation techniques you can use to help reduce anger, such as meditation, yoga, and prayer. You can also use a program for the systematic desensitization I mentioned earlier. This is where you desensitize your entire body, one part at a time, systematically. You can find examples of this technique online.

**TAKE A TIME-OUT**: Sometimes, in the heat of the battle, it is difficult to find a pause button, that little break from the anger you are experiencing. A great coping device is to remove yourself from the physical space where the anger is occurring, if you can. This helps provide that little break that can help your body, emotions, and your mind to reset and begin to detach from the angry episode.

**IDENTIFY AND RESPOND**: As mentioned, you can usually feel when you are about to get angry. At this time, you can identify that something is already happening. This is when your intellect still has a bit of control over what is happening. This is where you can decide to do something other than get angry, such as leaving the situation, attempting to broker a solution or using one of these coping strategies.

**POSITIVE INTERNAL LANGUAGE:** Anger is almost always accompanied by negative internal language. This often translates into negative and angry behaviors and, at times, violence. Positive language like "I am not going to let this bother me," "I am better than this," and "There are other ways to deal with this" begin to reverse the negative internal drive for anger and put you in a position for more intelligent thoughts and behaviors. Very often, the way we speak to ourselves is what we are telling ourselves to do. If you're telling yourself to get angry, you will. Conversely, if you are telling yourself to do something that will keep you from getting angry, you just might.

**SET BOUNDARIES:** Setting boundaries can help you avoid angry episodes. A boundary example might be "I'm not going to remain in situations that cause me to become emotional or angry. I will leave those situations as soon as I understand that I might get angry." Set your boundaries to avoid or leave potentially anger-provoking situations. This can help you establish a plan that can be called upon when necessary.

**KNOW WHEN TO DISENGAGE:** Everyone has a boiling point, and it is important to disengage—that is, remove yourself from the situation before you reach the boiling point. A boiling point can be the trigger that moves you into an angry episode, or it can be an identifier to let you know that it's time to leave. Usually, past angry episodes are good boiling-point indicators, since you know what happened when you reached your boiling point in those episodes They can help you set your point of disengagement for potential future episodes.

**MAKE THE DECISION:** A hallmark of human behavior is when we finally decide to do something. Then, we can take the appropriate steps to turn that decision into action. As simple as it sounds, deciding to stop using anger and being firm about that decision sets the stage for a plan to reduce using anger in your life. You can't do something until you decide to do it.

**GET HELP:** One of the most important coping strategies to deal with your anger is to deal with it before it controls your life. If you are angry and have been unsuccessful in trying to reduce it in your life, a professional counselor can help you address any issues that may be causing the anger. They will also help you learn to work with coping mechanisms along the way. Sometimes, the best coping device is the one where you learn more about yourself, your anger, and how to reduce it's influence over your life.

## MIXING AND MATCHING

As you saw in Part Two, there are many types of anger. It should not be a surprise that attempting to use one coping strategy might fall short in your attempts to either hold back your anger or to address someone else's. There are so many ways anger can manifest in someone's life. Rarely, if ever, is there only one cause for anger. There may have been initial circumstances that caused the anger to develop, but along the way, it attaches itself to other life circumstances. Therefore, to reduce anger should use a multifaceted coping approach. For example, if someone is dealing with rapid-onset anger, coping devices like time-outs, exercise, and getting professional help may apply. With passive-aggressive anger, setting boundaries and positive internal language can be more helpful.

If you have read other books in The Fix Yourself Empowerment Series, you probably noticed that I use more examples in this book to help illustrate important points. This is because anger, unlike anxiety and depression, tends to be explosive and can put you in a position to react fast. Angry expressions can cause severe damage not only to the person using it but also to whatever their anger is directed at. Here is an example to help you understand how to use coping devices to help you reduce anger's impact on your life:

Hannah is a twenty-eight-year-old architect. She was just promoted from a draftsperson's position in an architectural firm. Hannah is the oldest of three girls and comes from a family with a history of angry outbursts. Hannah's father is a low-key businessman, and her mother has wrestled with alcoholism for most of her adult life. One of her sisters also has a drinking problem. Hannah does not abuse alcohol, but from time to time, she can display a short fuse.

Hannah understands this and has been in a counseling program for five months. She and her counselor are working on some coping mechanisms to help her avoid or at least reduce some of the angry episodes. Hannah's mother's alcoholism is a strong undercurrent for her anger. She is resentful and, at times, has been vengeful with her mother. She does not live with her mother anymore, but they do talk on the phone almost every day.

Six months ago, Hannah and her mother got into a dreadful argument, where both became angry. The argument became personal and evolved into a pushing episode. This is the first time Hannah ever put her hands on her mother. During her life, Hannah was emotionally, verbally, and on a few occasions, physically abused by her mother. She has never been able to work through this, and everything came out in that argument. This was Hannah's motivating reason to schedule her initial counseling appointment.

As Hannah and her counselor continued to work on the trauma from her family life, her counselor decided to teach her some coping devices and strategies to help her through periods of emotional anger and to offset the potential for any angry episodes. Work has always been a positive outlet for Hannah, but last month, the company promoted a new draftsperson who is a year younger than Hannah. He is a traditional male, has his own anger issues, and tends to belittle Hannah, feeling that he is more intelligent and a better architect than she is.

Hannah knows that this person has his own issues and has discussed this with her counselor. Regardless, she needs to refrain from expressing any anger in her workplace, since her job is so important to her. Considering Hannah's background, her counselor has advised that she begin to use more positive internal language, refrain from making vengeful plans as she does with her mother, exercise more often, and to focus on her breathing program.

These coping strategies began to reduce the urge to express her anger, but she still felt that more was needed. Her counselor added self-soothing techniques and imagery to her plan. Hannah is meditating twice a day and is using some imagery to help establish a calm place when she meditates. She has been doing this for about a month and is noticing that, overall, she is feeling more relaxed. She is also removing herself from any situation with the other employee unless it happens to be work-related.

Hannah will continue to work with her counselor to help her settle issues from her family life. In the meantime, the coping mechanisms she has included as part of Hannah's therapeutic plan are helping her to avoid angry outbursts at work, and are also helping her to be calmer in her daily life.

This is an example of using coping strategies to reduce the impact of anger in your world and to create a happier life with reduced anger.

## POSITIVE EFFECTS OF COPING TECHNIQUES

Working your way through angry undercurrents and current life situations can take some time. The undercurrents and the thinking and reacting that they produce, especially over time, can train the brain to use more angry techniques to settle current life situations. Using coping techniques to address the possibility of angry outbursts has three positive effects:

1. They can be a stopgap measure to help reduce anger while triggers and pain emanating from past and current circumstances are being addressed.

2. They can help you create an improved style of life since your brain will accommodate the changes in the way you are thinking and behaving, and you can begin using these types of strategies not only to address anger but also to enhance the quality of your entire life.

3. It can keep you from reacting to anger-provoking people and situations while they are occurring.

We can all learn to more efficiently cope with situations that cause us to become emotional and react with anger. Coping devices are simply strategies for healthy living. Sometimes the strategy is introduced in response to some negative circumstances we may be experiencing, but at other times, they can be incorporated into a healthy living plan. Your brain will adjust to the changes you are making, and if you stay consistent, you can expect to experience the improvements you are looking for.

 **TIME TO TAKE ACTION**

1. Familiarize yourself with the various types of coping skills. Discuss how to best use them with someone close to you.

2. Select two or three coping skills and attempt to incorporate them into your daily life. Try to use them several times per day.

3. If you find it difficult to remember to practice your coping skills regularly, ask for help from a family member or a friend, or you can set a reminder on your phone.

4. If you are still having trouble turning to coping skills instead of reacting, schedule an appointment with a professional counselor who can help you identify which coping skills may work best for you and how you can efficiently begin to use them.

## 🎯 Driving It Home

Anger can take so much from your life. Learning to reduce its impact on your life can take time. This doesn't mean you will remain angry until you finally settle past issues and present-day triggers. As you work with coping devices, and the other information and advice I am providing you with, you will gradually see a reduction in your anger, and in your angry thoughts and actions. Involving yourself with a professional counselor is also a great step. While you are working through those old issues, begin to incorporate some coping strategies to reduce your anger and change the way it works its way through your body, your emotions, and your mind.

**YOUR DECLARATION IS:** *I will learn to cope with my anger so I can be a happier and more peaceful person!*

## Onward

The language you use to talk to yourself internally can have an impact on the way you think and behave. In the next chapter, I examine how negative internal language can help set you up for angry outbursts, what you can do to stop using it, and create a way of speaking to yourself that moves you away from anger and into a happier way to think.

CHAPTER 20

# Internal Language: Positive Self Talk

*Make a conscious decision to avoid all forms of negative language. The way you speak to yourself creates the person you will become.*

**PROCESSES TO EMPLOY:** Brutal Honesty, I Over E, Present/Understand/Fix, Slowing Down Life's Pace, Internal Focus, Fact-Finding, Warm Confrontation, Positive Language Reciprocity, Communication, Conflict Resolution, Listening, Living in the Moment, Settling Past Issues, Life Inventory

IN THE PAST FOUR CHAPTERS, I PROVIDED YOU with information you can use to reduce the impact of anger in your life. One of the most powerful tools that can influence whether you continue to be angry or whether you reduce anger's hold over you is your internal language. I define "internal language" as *the nonverbal language used to express feelings, define people and circumstances, play out internal scenarios, and formulate plans to address real-life situations.*

Everyone with a functioning brain uses internal language. Unless you have suffered traumatic brain injury or some other neurological disorder or if you are in a coma, you are speaking internally. This occurs when you think. You think with language. This occurs when words are strung together to produce a thought. Those words strung together can explain what we are thinking and feeling, and at times, they can direct our thoughts and actions.

Typically, you spend a significantly greater amount of time in your own mind than you do in the external world. If you are spending a large amount of your internal time with negative language, it creates a negative version of yourself and influences you to live that way. When, however, you learn to use language to be a positive thinker, it becomes an ally for you. You are what you think, so you need to be thinking healthy thoughts, as you will see as we proceed.

We use language to state and clarify our positions and opinions, to connect with others, and to gain information in a wide variety of formats. We can instill fear with our words, or we can express love. We can speak from our hearts, or we can lie through our teeth. We can draw people in, or we can push them way out. We can use language to educate, or we can use it to confuse. We can speak with straightforwardness, or we can be conniving and manipulative. Language is one of the more powerful tools you will use as your life unfolds, and it has a tremendous influence regarding whether or not you will be an angry person.

## THE INNER VOICE

Language is a powerful internal influencer. You use language to communicate with yourself, just as you do with others. Language is not only the byproduct of what you think but also helps create, define, and redefine the way you think. An angry person is more likely to have negative thoughts. If your internal language is negative about yourself, the people in your life, or your environment, you may come to believe what you are thinking and may adopt that as the default way you think about others, the world you are living in, and yourself.

If, however, you make a conscious effort to talk to yourself using positive language, your words can help you create positive feelings about yourself. The way you think and the way you feel are so intimately interwoven. Likewise, the way you think and feel usually equals the way you behave. So, the language you use, primarily with yourself, will eventually translate into who you are and how you represent yourself to the rest of the world.

## Master and Slave

Language does not only describe what your brain thinks and feels but also often tells your brain *what* to think and feel. Language can tell your brain to feel good about something or someone, or it can define your world using aggressive and negative terminology. Sometimes those thoughts are consciously applied, but over time, the way you speak to yourself can become your personal linguistic autopilot. Those undercurrents first introduced in Chapter 5 have much to do with the way you think about yourself and others. Past undercurrents that can cause you to be angry create an internal language that, though it may not focus specifically on those past events, uses that negative energy to create an internal dialogue that can be negative and angry.

Positive internal language, conversely, paves the way for the type of thinking that coincides with a positive self-image, respect for others, and a productive way of living that sets the stage for warm and loving relationships and personal productivity. It is not influenced by past traumas and angry undercurrents and routinely attempts to access positive energy. Positive internal language looks at the brighter side and always attempts to arrive at solutions to life problems.

The following table includes examples of positive and negative internal language.

## INTERNAL LANGUAGE COMPARISON

| Positive Internal Language | Negative Internal Language |
|---|---|
| Things are good in my life. | I hate my life. |
| I can do that with a little effort. | Nothing I do ever turns out right. |
| I think people feel good about me. | No one likes me. |
| I have what I need to succeed. | I never get what I need. |
| People are inherently good. | People are inherently evil. |
| I feel good about myself. | I don't like myself. |
| If you give people a chance, they will come through. | If you give people an opportunity, they will hurt you. |

As you can see, positive internal language defines what a person may be feeling and sets the course for what a person may do. If you have unresolved past issues, operate with passive-aggressive and/or retaliatory tendencies, use anger to hide your insecurities and/or to appear more righteous, or even if your anger is a product of physiological circumstances, your intolerance and agitation levels can increase and thereby affect the way you speak to yourself.

## Setting the Internal Record Straight

Sometimes, internal language can be used in an attempt to settle scores or even arrive at solutions to problems with other people and external issues that instigate anger for you. Negative internal language isn't only expressed in simple statements like "I don't like that person" or "I would like to hurt them." Sometimes it is an extended dialogue where the negative internal language takes the form of a conversation. When this happens, it may be for the following reasons:

1. It may serve to settle the score with another person through an argument where your internal language guides you to victory.

2. To provide what seems like immediate solutions to problems that create fear, resentment, victimization, and anger.

3. To address obsessive thinking in what seems to be a productive way.

This type of internal dialogue does little if anything to resolve situations. Since it is expressed as internal anger, it has no real solution-oriented path to follow. It is often expressed instead of having a productive face-to-face dialogue with the other person. In Chapter 18, I discussed the middle ground anger can take where instead of standing strong and fighting or running from the situation, there is that middle ground where something else needs to be done. Very often, that middle ground is attempting to engage in a productive dialogue. Instead of doing something like working for a solution, people often find themselves engaged in a negative angry internal argument that is neither productive nor efficient. It does little to address the issue at hand.

As I mentioned, angry internal language can be comprised of simple angry statements, or it can evolve into something more prolonged such as an actual internal quasi-confrontation. The more common simple statements can include:

- I really hate that person.
- If I have the opportunity, I am going to hurt that person.
- Try that again and see what happens.
- I'm going to kill that miserable SOB.

For some people, those simple statements can evolve into a full-blown internal dialogue, as I mentioned earlier. This is where the simple statements can be initiated and expanded to include an angry and threatening internal conversation. For most people, when this happens, it is a product of their inability to stop the obsessive thoughts. As this is happening, the body stays rigid and primed for action, the emotions are heightened as though the conversation with the other person is actually happening, and the intellect is using threats in an angry internal linguistic format.

In *The Fix Yourself Handbook*, I describe this behavior in greater detail. The following is an excerpt from that book:

### Ghost Screaming

Sometimes the emotions that stem from not confronting someone can become so intense that we begin to talk to ourselves about the problem, with considerable emotion. I call this behavior *ghost screaming*. This is where we begin to have emotionally laden conversations with the person we aren't confronting. We begin by rehearsing what we want to say to the other person. Soon, we are in a heated debate with someone who isn't there.

Ghost screaming is nothing more than a misguided internal attempt to organize the information in a situation with the hopes of bringing it to some type of conclusion. It is our way of trying to put closure on a situation that requires confronting another individual, without the confrontation.

Ghost screaming is an emotional outcry. This behavior occurs when we have become so frustrated with a person, or some situation that we can't see our way out of it. We may anticipate that the other person will not cooperate, or that the situation, for whatever reason, is not fixable. The real explanation, however, is that we cannot stop thinking about it, and we are afraid to confront the other person peacefully.

People often either run away from confrontations or create some pseudo-intellectual explanation as to why confronting the situation won't work. In the end, however, the situation doesn't change, we continue to scream, and we are becoming more frustrated, angry, and very unhappy with ourselves.

An angry internal dialogue is nothing more than a

continuation of the anger that can be so destructive in your life. There is a cycle of anger it perpetuates, which does nothing to relieve anger, and only makes it that much worse. Look at it this way. You are an angry person. You tend to act out in situations that irritate you, make you feel threatened, or that you can use to manipulate others. When you are not with other people, you continue your angry venture by supporting it with an internal dialogue which is also angry. Now, without any real break from your angry disposition, you are back in the world, and you are getting angry again. This cycle can repeat itself over and over again.

## THE INTERNAL HIGH ROAD

Let's explore the angry thought-to-action-to-thought cycle. You may have had a problem with anger for a reasonable amount of time, maybe all your life. You are supporting your angry lifestyle with an internal dialogue that is also angry. What would happen if you start making changes to that internal dialogue? Specifically, what would happen if you begin training your brain to stay away from angry statements and conversations, and replace them with a dialogue that is a bit more positive?

For as long as you have been using angry internal language, you have provided your mind with the time it took to adjust to this linguistic format and the angry actions that may follow. Your brain did not simply begin to speak in angry terms and then you began to display angry behaviors. This has been a neurological training program that you have provided for your brain, and as I have stressed, your brain will learn what you want it to do and help you live that way.

The method to stop the cycle is to retrain your brain to think in ways that are not angry. This is a two-step process:

- As angry thoughts enter your mind, consciously say, "I am not going to think about this," and then shut that thought down.

- It is important to replace the angry thought with something more positive like a statement that describes something positive in your life or where you are at that time.

The approach seems simple, but when you think about it, this is exactly the opposite of what you have been doing for so long. Initially, you began to think angry thoughts and did not challenge those thoughts. Your mind may have developed simple angry statements into much longer angry internal conversations. To reverse the process of continuing to think angry thoughts, the logical first step is to quickly stop that particular thought. Instead of developing it, you terminate it. Expect it to start all over again, sometimes very soon. When that happens, you simply repeat the process. In the beginning, you will do this repeatedly. As your mind adjusts—and it will—you will need to do it less often.

To help your mind adjust to its new way of thinking, you need to replace the thought you are terminating with something more positive. This allows your mind to stop thinking the angry thought and directs your mind to a new thought without angry overtones. You are asking your mind to produce positive linguistic energy. Doing these two steps repeatedly over time can help you train your brain to move away from negative thinking, replace it with more productive thoughts, and help you reduce the urge to turn angry thinking into angry behavior.

Practicing these two steps will not change much *initially*. The key to any training format, one that is designed to help you learn a new approach, is something I have been teaching for many years. *Learning is a function of repetition over time.* You are not going to change your angry thinking quickly. Angry thoughts do not begin to occur overnight, and you will not change them overnight either. As your mind needs time to adjust to your angry language, it also needs time to adjust to your new approach. How much time it takes depends on how intense your angry language is, how often you use it, how often it gives way to angry behaviors, and how committed you are to changing it. However, if you remain committed to repeating these two steps consistently, your brain's learning time can be significantly reduced.

To help you replace angry thoughts with positive thinking, it is a good idea to write down a list of all the positive people and things in your life. Sometimes, when you are involved in angry thoughts, it can be difficult to turn your attention to something more positive. Writing down a list of positive people and things in your life can make that thought transition just a bit easier. When you are thinking angry thoughts, take out your list and review it. Another way to help you with this part of the process is to look around the room or the environment you are currently in and find anything you can say something positive about. It could be a nice car, the way someone is dressed, a flower, or the way another person goes out of their way to be nice to you.

Your goal is to reduce the amount of angry thinking as much as you possibly can. Not only does angry thinking potentially turn into angry behavior, but it also keeps you in a negative frame of mind. When I discussed physiological anger in Chapter 8, I told you how being angry changes your body physically. Another advantage of learning how to change your internal dialogue into a more positive presentation is that when you reduce your anger, your body will feel that much better.

Reducing the number of angry inner dialogues you have each day is a huge step for you as you begin to change not only the way you think but also the way you behave. Physically, your body will feel better; emotionally, you will reduce the overwhelming feelings you are experiencing; intellectually, you will experience more clarity; and spiritually, you will find it easier to connect with the deeper parts of yourself. Try to let go of the angry thoughts. Stay committed to the steps provided in this chapter. If you do, your brain will adjust, and your life will change.

**TIME TO TAKE ACTION**

1. Keep an informal log of how often you think angry thoughts and how involved they become. This will help you understand what you were doing at the time, and may give you some information regarding why these angry thoughts are occurring.

2. Make a list of all the positive people and things in your life. Study that list and try to commit it to memory.

3. Each day, as angry thoughts begin, terminate the thought by telling yourself, "I am not going to continue thinking about this." This will help you begin to redirect your thought process.

4. To redirect your thoughts, focus on your list of positive people and things in your life or what you can see around you. Replace the angry thoughts with positive thoughts.

5. If you are unable to stop thinking angry thoughts, it might be because you are struggling with obsessive thinking. The inability to stop angry thoughts suggests that you may need help. Make an appointment with a professional counselor to help you work your way through this.

 **DRIVING IT HOME**

Anger can change the way you feel about yourself and put you in a position to believe that it will never change. Past angry episodes may have created relationship problems and other forms of collateral damage. This may cause you to believe that you are not worthy of the good things life has to offer. Nothing could be further from the truth. Take the time to retrain your brain. Help your mind to learn to stop negative thinking and replace it with more positive thinking. If you do, in time, you may find the peace you have always been looking for.

**YOUR DECLARATION IS:** *I will stop thinking angry thoughts, and I will create more peace in my life!*

 **ONWARD**

A lot of anger has to do with not letting go of something that has happened or something that continues to happen. Holding on to grudges and past pains seems to give anger a rational reason to be expressed; rather, it provides an opportunity to practice forgiveness. In the next chapter, I discuss how to incorporate forgiveness into your recovery from anger as another ally in your fight to remove this nagging nemesis from your life.

CHAPTER 21

# Letting Go: Understanding Forgiveness

*Nothing says, "You will not hurt me any longer" better than forgiveness. Stop taking the poison—forgive and let go.*

**PROCESSES TO EMPLOY:** Brutal Honesty, I Over E, Present/Understand/Fix, Slowing Down Life's Pace, Internal Focus, Fact-Finding, Internal Focus, Forgiveness, Humility, Gratitude, Faith, Living in the Moment, Settling Past Issues, Life Inventory

AS YOU NOW UNDERSTAND, UNDERCURRENTS ARE BELOW-THE-SURFACE anger motivators that keep us focused on either past or present people or situations that have caused us pain. They can instigate anger or, at times, be a reaction to it. Undercurrents can also be an outgrowth of damage you may have caused to others and the guilt that arises from those actions.

Sometimes memories of abuse or traumatic situations can cause you to be angry, and that anger may be displayed in situations that are not specifically related to the past trauma. Other times, you may know exactly what you are angry about, and this can be the catalyst for present-day anger. It doesn't matter what occurred in your past; it could spark any of the types of anger I discuss in this book.

When someone has done something to you that has caused you pain and you feel it may have had a profound effect on your life, it is easy to become angry and carry this anger with you. This is where the obsessive thinking, the ghost screaming (see page 134), and the ideation about getting revenge discussed in Chapter 19 come from. When you look at the progression of anger from past situations and from people who may have abused you, carrying the pain along with you continues to give it life. What's more, it can make it feel like you are experiencing the pain all over again. It is so important to take the steps to rid yourself of these past demons before they define who you are and how you live your life in the present.

## FORGIVING AND LETTING GO

When you are angry, forgiving the other person without some form of retribution, revenge, retaliation, or at least a heartfelt and sincere apology from the other person seems to be a farfetched and unrealistic suggestion. This person did something to you, caused you a great deal of pain, and may have altered the course of your life to some degree, and you are simply going to forgive, forget, and go on like nothing happened? That's not exactly what I am talking about.

As I'm defining it here, "forgiving" *is the result of a step-by-step understanding and systematic removal of negative energy and self-defeating thoughts with a plan to ensure that the wrongdoing won't happen again.* Forgiveness is a process that can restore you to intellectual and emotional sanity and ultimately support your internal balance. When your anger motivates you to consider ways of getting even or inflicting pain on the other person, it is you who must continue to live with memories about the incident you are keeping alive with your anger.

People who have inflicted pain on a person they feel hurt them often report that even though they got even with the other person, it didn't take away their anger. It is almost impossible to stop feeling angry by using anger. The problem with using anger to get even at others is twofold:

1. It does not relieve you of the anger you feel.

2. It enhances your feeling that, no matter what you do, you will continue to be angry about what happened to you.

Exacting your revenge or retaliation only to realize that it does little to remove the anger from your life keeps those angry thoughts active and predisposes you to the angry behaviors they can instigate. Also, since you are still angry and cannot resolve the anger by directly attacking the other person, you are more likely to continue being angry, targeting your angry outburst on those around you. Innocent people often suffer because someone in their life could not let go of past pain or trauma, felt that they had a right to be angry, and with or without knowing it, displayed their anger toward the people in their lives who had nothing to do with what occurred.

Forgiving and letting go is not designed to let the other person off the hook. In many cases, the person who inflicted the pain does not understand the gravity of their actions. This may not apply to everyone who causes pain for someone else, but many people either don't know what they did or don't understand how much pain it caused. Many angry people have never confronted the other person to let them know what they did and what impact it had on their lives. Instead, they internalize the pain, carry the anger, and introduce it in situations and with other people that had nothing to do with the problem.

## THE PLAN FOR FORGIVING OTHERS AND LETTING GO

Simply saying, "I am going to forgive them and not hold them accountable for what they did to me," is extremely difficult for an angry person, so any plan to forgive and let go should have two basic components:

1. It should present a *constructive* way to hold the other person accountable and let them know what kind of damage they caused.

2. It should include a plan to remove or at least significantly reduce the pain caused by that person's actions.

Constructively holding someone else accountable is accomplished by confronting the other person peacefully and telling them clearly and plainly what they did and why it caused in your life. When someone does something to you and you do not confront them, the sense that there's unfinished business keeps the anger flowing. Confronting the other person allows you to take that internal anger and channel it in a constructive way to let the other person know what they did, what it did to you, and how you will never allow that to occur again. In Chapter 16 of *The Fix Yourself Handbook*, I discussed how to peacefully confront others about situations you feel are important.

You have no control over what the other person will say or do. If you think the situation could become volatile, have people who can support you by your side. The goal is *not* to initiate an angry confrontation. It is simply to verbally, peacefully, and constructively set the record straight so that the other person understands their offensive act and knows your boundaries moving forward. Regardless of how the other person responds to your peaceful confrontation, the matter is no longer locked inside you, making you feel horrible and causing collateral damage and pain in other areas of your life.

Having now peacefully confronted the other person, it is time to begin the process of removing the pain and the anger it caused from your life. Keep in mind that being angry about what someone did to you may be appropriate, but it does not justify taking anger out on innocent people. Your first order of business is to set this score straight with anyone who may have been a victim of your angry outbursts. If apologies are necessary, apologize. This helps remove any undercurrent of guilt you may have regarding your angry reaction and helps you repair any damage you may have done. So, forgiving is a process that helps you reduce the impact of what someone may have done to you, but it is also about forgiving yourself for what you may have done to other people. You cannot forgive yourself for what you have done to someone else until you apologize and make amends with them. Isn't that what you want from the person who hurt you? Regardless of whether it is about something someone did to you or something you did to someone else, it still creates negative energy and affects the way you feel about yourself and how you will live the rest of your life.

The next part of the letting go process is to put that past trauma in perspective. This is where you do a thorough review of all the events that led up to your pain, where you discuss your feelings about what occurred with someone you trust, and where you begin to create your movement forward with less emotional pain and a happier, more productive direction. This is also where, if you are having difficulty letting go, the services of a professional counselor can help. They can help you work through the pain and establish new directions in your life.

## THE PLAN FOR FORGIVING YOURSELF AND LETTING GO

You can still be angry, even without past trauma. Sometimes that has a physiological etiology, sometimes it can be what you learned from others, or it may be the way you have trained your brain to think and react. Regardless of how it began, angry people can hurt other people. At times, it is subtle anger (e.g., passive-aggressive anger), and other times, it can be in-your-face anger (e.g., volatile anger). The type of anger doesn't matter. Anger causes pain.

You may feel as though the anger you express after someone hurt you may be justified. You may also feel that what they did was purposeful and caused you pain. Angry people have a way of blaming other people, events, and objects for their anger. It is interesting to note that people who are not angry do not respond with anger most of the time in these situations. They try to work through it, and already know that they don't want this situation to become a nagging part of their lives.

This is not the case with people who are dealing with anger. They often feel that their anger is justified, and in the process, they inflict their anger on other people. If you are working through anger and want to be able to reduce anger in your life, it is important to come to terms with yourself as being a person who might have caused someone else pain in much the same way the person you are angry with did to you. If you know you have done something wrong and have not made amends to a person who was hurt by your actions, you may carry guilt, and this is a self-damaging way to continue living.

Perpetually angry people have a way of apologizing and then repeating the angry behavior. This has nothing at all to do with forgiving and letting go. Forgiving is not a quick fix. It is a step-by-step process that repairs any damage done to another person, includes remorse for your actions and a plan to never do it again. Say you have done something you believe is significant enough to have caused someone pain, and this has damaged your feelings about yourself. You may be having difficulty moving past the event. The "sticking spot" regarding what has occurred can present itself in four ways:

1. It can cause you to feel sad and experience guilt and shame.

2. You can use your defenses such as denial, rationalization, and intellectualizing what you have done to make yourself feel better.

3. You can blame others for the way you feel and what you have done.

4. You can begin to either consciously or unconsciously punish yourself for what you have done since you feel that you deserve sanctions that are commensurate with the seriousness of the deed.

The features of the plan to address accountability and, subsequently, your ability to forgive yourself are:

1. You must first understand that there is negative energy attached to what you have done. That damage could be to yourself only or there may be others involved.

2. You need to be factual and honest in your representation of what happened. There are no excuses or extenuating circumstances.

3. Make a list of everyone who may have been affected by your actions. Then, be responsible enough, humble enough, and brave enough to make amends with those people. This may include expressions of sorrow, and you need to make a concerted effort to

understand what your actions caused them to experience. It may also include what you may need to do to help repair the damage caused by your actions.

4. You need to consider the dynamics of your thoughts and emotions and how they led you to behave as you did. This is extremely important so that you can understand what you did, why you did it, and how to avoid ever doing it again. *Your ability to forgive yourself will only be as strong as your commitment to never repeating the behavior.*

## IT TAKES COURAGE

Most people overlook forgiveness when it comes to anger. Either you are so angry about what someone has done to you or you are too angry to realize what you have done to someone else. Forgiveness is often seen as a sign of weakness. Anger can make you feel as though you are more powerful than the event or person who caused your anger. This can get in the way of the self-examination process, which is so essential to forgiving and letting go.

Forgiving and letting go require more courage than harboring and expressing anger. As I mentioned as far back as Chapter 1, anger is often an outgrowth of fear and insecurities. Unfortunately, since anger is often driven by hormonal and neurotransmitter imbalance, it creates the misconception that you can rise above whatever caused your fear and pain. Anger may fool you into believing that you are more powerful, but that will never be the case. Continuing to give life to anger's mask of fear and insecurity stands in the way of your ability to be introspective and to understand the power of forgiveness. It also negates your ability to move away from the anger that has directed the course of your life for so long.

Many people claim to have forgiven people who have hurt them without having taken the steps outlined earlier to make that happen. As I mentioned in Chapter 20, it can be difficult to confront someone with something that can be intellectually and emotionally challenging. This difficulty also applies to forgiving someone. Instead of confronting them, it is easier to just say, "The matter is in the past, and I'm letting it go." Try not to fall into this trap. If you do not take the steps to fully let go of the past or forgive yourself for something you may have done, the negative energy associated with these events will continue to move forward with you. All it takes is one simple triggering event to activate the anger you thought you let go of.

Forgiving and letting go can help restore your brain, your emotions, and your body to a more relaxed state and provide the foundation for you to alleviate past pain and move ahead in your life as a healthier person—physically, emotionally, intellectually, and spiritually. Some people find that connecting with God or a higher power through prayer or other spiritual practices is helpful. You can also include your forgiving dialogue in your meditations and along with your daily breathing exercises. This will help you express them while you are taking steps to reduce their impact on your life.

Forgiving others and letting go of the aftereffects of your original painful or traumatic circumstances opens the door for better feelings about yourself and warmer relationships with other people. Be willing to face the issues that have caused your anger. Consider the processes of forgiving yourself and others presented in this chapter and open the door to a more peaceful, more loving, and more productive life.

**TIME TO TAKE ACTION**

1. Make a list of all the people in your life you may have hurt and prioritize that list with those who you hurt most on the top of the list.

2. Make a second list of any past pain from others or traumatic situations and prioritize that list, starting with the person or event that felt most painful.

3. For all the people you hurt, be willing to sincerely apologize to them, and then use the format I present in this chapter to help you forgive yourself and let go to address the pain you have caused them.

4. Using your second list, decide whether you can confront anyone who hurt you in the past. Sometimes this is difficult, and your second decision is whether you may need help to do this.

5. Make an appointment with a professional counselor if you have not done so. Forgiveness requires brutal honesty and will take you deep into some past issues that may be very painful. It is a good idea to have a counselor help you with this process.

 **DRIVING IT HOME**

Forgiving others and letting go of the pain they caused you purges you of the toxic and negative energy that leads to an angry style of life. The person who caused the pain or the event that was traumatic for you did enough damage to you. You don't want to continue to move that negative energy forward with you as your life continues. Decide to rid yourself of these painful thoughts and feelings. Be brave enough to forgive and let go, and you will be taking the yet another step in becoming the happy person you always wanted to be.

**YOUR DECLARATION IS:** *I will forgive and let go so I can be happy!*

 **ONWARD**

If the cause of someone's anger is not efficiently defined, attempting to move past it and trying to incorporate new strategies are often met with failure—or, at the very least, internal resistance. Anger can be difficult and complicated condition to reduce. This is why I have discussed working with the professional counselor throughout the book. In the next chapter, I discuss how professional counseling can be beneficial for moving away from anger and toward a happier new you. I will also be discussing how to select and work with a professional counselor.

CHAPTER 22

# Getting Help: Trust on a Higher Level

*There is no honor in burying your pain and suffering in the depths of loneliness and desperation. There is no shame in asking for help.*

**PROCESSES TO EMPLOY:** Brutal Honesty, I Over E, Present/Understand/Fix, Slowing Down Life's Pace, Internal Focus, Fact-Finding, Living in the Moment, Settling Past Issues, Learning to Be Comfortable with Being Uncomfortable, Trust, Humility, Gratitude, Faith, Risk-Taking, Goal-Setting, Sustained Learning, Belief

AS FAR BACK AS CHAPTER 3, I suggested including a professional counselor in your efforts to help remove anger from your world. I discussed how embattled anger can make you feel and how anger is destroying your life. I have also discussed how anger robs you of your self-esteem and connects with the parts of your life that may include guilt, shame, poor self-worth, and collateral damage. All too often, people with anger have difficulty taking the advice of others, so getting help can be difficult for them.

For most people, there is an arrogant component that develops as anger begins to infiltrate your mind and your emotions. "Arrogance" is typically defined as *overbearing pride or haughtiness, exaggerating or disposed to exaggerate one's own worth or importance often in an overbearing manner, or showing an offensive attitude of superiority.* Some of the qualities displayed by arrogant people include:

- They believe they are smarter.
- They show off around others.
- They talk over you.
- They can be condescending.
- They are argumentative.
- They are constantly seeking attention.
- They seem to need excessive praise.
- They routinely give unsolicited advice.
- They exhibit high competitiveness.
- They consider others as their adversaries.
- They believe they know it all.
- They belittle others.
- They are disrespectful communicators.
- They refuse to admit mistakes.
- They reject others' feedback.
- They display a sense of entitlement.
- They can have a superiority complex.

As you can see from the list, the qualities typically displayed by arrogant people might make it difficult for them to be vulnerable, truthful, willing to admit when they are wrong, be humble, and take advice from other people. Angry people do find themselves in counseling situations, but this is usually in the aftermath of some crisis where they feel as though there is much to lose.

It is important to keep in mind that many angry people come from backgrounds where trauma and abuse were thrust upon them. They often have little trust for other people, and throughout their lives, they may have experienced pain, ridicule, and invalidation when they did try to open up. As a result, angry people use arrogance, not so much for profit, but as a defense mechanism to keep from coming face to face with their actions, for the problems with self-esteem and self-worth, and to put intellectual and emotional distance between themselves and others. In cases of physical abuse, arrogance may also be used as a shield to keep people from physically hurting them. As time goes on, arrogant people may see some profit in their methods, but arrogance is still an insecure protection device for them.

If you are dealing with anger in your life and others in your life have commented on your arrogance or any of the behaviors associated with arrogance, it may be time to look at whether or not you *are* being arrogant and why this is happening. We all use our defense systems to protect ourselves from intellectual and emotional assaults from others. Arrogance may be one of those defense mechanisms, and may be useful in keeping others from hurting you because it also causes people to feel as though you think you are better than they are. They may respond by trying to put distance between you and themselves. As a result, many of the reasons for using arrogance may be exacerbated by your behavior.

Very few people want to get close to an arrogant person. The anger that stems from past traumas and from present circumstances in your life may make it difficult for you to let others close. Being arrogant might convince you that you have control over potentially damaging people and situations, but this is a false sense of empowerment, and as I mentioned in Chapter 1, its foundation is not strength but fear and security. Your attempts to convince the world that you have risen above them and that they cannot hurt you may be successful, but you may compromise their willingness to connect with and support you. As a result, you will continue to be an angry person, and you may find yourself alone in the process.

## SURRENDER, MINUS THE WHITE FLAG

Here is a revised definition of "arrogance": *Arrogance is an unrealistic and irrational view of oneself as being superior to others and is a compensatory defense to hide feelings of insecurity, fear, and questions regarding one's self-worth.* If one possesses real qualities of superior intellect, internal control, and the ability to control one's internal attributes and external environment, there is little, if any, reason to use the behaviors displayed by an arrogant person. Feeling secure with oneself does not require external displays. One who is emotionally stable and intellectually confident understands the bigger picture and knows that expressions of arrogance will only cause problems with other people.

If you are using some of the qualities of an arrogant person and cannot stop on your own, it is a signal to yourself that you have unresolved issues and that you are trying to rise above those issues by attempting to present an outward persona that is not consistent with the real circumstances of your life. If you are using these strategies, you are probably afraid, feeling vulnerable, keeping people from doing any possible harm to you, have unresolved past issues, or are caught in an angry web that you do not know how to free yourself from. If this is the case, counseling will not hurt you; there is no submissive surrender involved, you are not going to lose yourself in it, and you are not weak if you take this step.

*The Fix Your Depression Handbook* includes a chapter on how to obtain professional help, how to find the right person who can help you deal with your problems, and how to begin to involve yourself in a counseling program. I provided the keys for selecting a counselor to meet your needs and how to present the initial questions you should have about the counselor and the counseling experience to help ease your mind about taking this essential step. Since finding a counselor and involving yourself in a counseling program does not change regardless of the emotional issue you are dealing with, I present some of that information here as it applies to your anger. If you cannot reduce anger's grip on you, you may need help. However, you should not be expected to do this without a helping hand to get you started. What follows is adapted from *The Fix Your Depression Handbook.*

## FINDING YOUR PERSONAL COUNSELOR

Throughout this book, you have seen how anger can turn your life into an aggressive and hostile place to live. I have also stressed that it does not have to be this way. If you are considering counseling, you may be making one of the biggest decisions of your life. You will be asking yourself to trust someone. This is not just trusting them with some small secret you don't want other people to know. This is about trusting them with the history of your life, those insecurities and undercurrents, and with the formulation of a plan to help you do things differently.

As anger begins to wreak havoc in your life and you begin to comprehend how much damage is being done to you and those around you, you may finally understand that you cannot reduce your angry feelings without help. You may understand that you need someone who knows what to do to get you through this. So, now it is time to decide who your personal counselor will be. You could ask friends or go online and pick someone, but there are some more informed ways to address this next important step.

Your first order of business is to make a list of your needs. These are the problems that need to be solved. This will give you information about what you need to change, what types of anger need to be addressed (refer to Part Two to identify your anger), and what areas of expertise your prospective counselor should possess. This list will also provide your counselor with a foundation from which to help you.

Keep in mind that you may be using several different types of anger. If you are not clear on which type(s) of anger is affecting your life, enlist the help of a trusted family member or a friend for fresh eyes on this step.

Your counselor should possess formal training in psychology or counseling. Avoid those with short-term educational program certificates. Many life coaches do good work, but anger is such an involved condition that you want to ensure that the person counseling you has a strong background in counseling dynamics, and especially in anger management and counseling techniques. In some cases, you may want a counselor with a medical background or who has the appropriate medical personnel in their professional network, especially if your anger is caused by a health problem.

Of most importance is your prospective counselor's understanding of and expertise in treating various types of anger. Many therapists, though they may be professional counselors or even licensed psychologists, may not have an in-depth background in treating anger and the past undercurrents that may support its use. Ask them if they understand the various types of anger and what to do about each.

In some cases, you may be more comfortable with someone who is older and perhaps a bit more seasoned in their profession. In other cases, gender may be a concern for you. If you are part of the LBGTQ community, you may want someone who understands your life dynamics. The location of the counselor's office and whether insurance is accepted are also legitimate concerns. Though these are all important factors, the most important skill this professional needs is a thorough understanding of the various types of anger and their ability to help you through yours.

The following steps can help you select the right counselor.

## The 7 Keys to Selecting Your Personal Counselor

1. Make sure the counselor has expertise in the dynamics and treatment of anger. The *Psychology Today* website is an excellent source for finding and securing a psychologist with anger-management expertise. Other pertinent information such as the type of insurance they take can be found there.

2. Match your counselor's abilities with your needs. Let friends and family members help you as you select your new counselor.

3. If possible, try to see the counselor in their office. If this is not possible, make sure that they can treat your anger using video conferencing platforms. During your initial session, ask them to explain how they will approach your online therapy sessions in a way that will help you.

4. Ask the counselor if they are members of professional associations like the American Psychological Association or the American

Counseling Association. You may even be able to verify their credentials through these associations.

5. Ask your primary care physician if they know anything about the counselor you are considering. You may even include your primary care physician in your search process and in your decision regarding which counselor to choose. They may have psychologists and professional counselors in their professional networks.

6. Make sure your counselor has a professional network in case you need referrals that are beyond the scope of their level of expertise. Examples may be attorneys, financial planning professionals, and medical professionals.

7. Be willing to schedule a consultation with a counselor you are considering without the commitment of continuing the counseling immediately. If you feel comfortable with them, that is a good first step. Ask them how they plan to help you work through your anger. Make sure you feel good about what you are experiencing during that first consultation.

### Questions to Ask a Prospective Counselor

Many people become anxious about questions to ask your counselor to get things started. They are not sure where to start or what questions to ask the counselor the first time they meet them. Here is a short checklist of questions to ask a counselor during your first consultation. These may be asked in your introductory telephone call with them, or in your first counseling session.

- Can I see your counseling credentials? They should be available to you.
- Can you describe your expertise regarding the dynamics and treatment of the various types of anger?
- Do you have affiliations with other professionals in case I need services in different areas?

- Do you also specialize in family counseling, and can I include members of my family in the sessions from time to time?
- Are you available for me in your office as well as in virtual counseling sessions?
- Are you available during off hours in case I need to contact you during an emergency?
- Do you take my insurance (if you have insurance), or is there a sliding scale for payments?

When these questions are answered, and you feel comfortable with proceeding with your counselor, tell them what you are experiencing, when it began, and how it is affecting your life. You don't have to go into detail. This just helps you start the dialogue. Your counselor will take it from there.

Selecting your personal counselor is not the monster you may think it is. Not selecting a counselor can leave you with no treatment options, and your anger may continue to negatively impact your life. In the counseling setting, your counselor can become your go-to person whom you can access not only when you are in crisis but also for everyday questions. In the counseling sessions, everything you discuss will be confidential, and this person can help you address some of those old traumas and painful situations, as well as people who have hurt you at various stages throughout your life. They will also help you use anger less in your life and assist you in repairing the damage your anger has caused.

Don't let your anger or your arrogance get in the way of making an intelligent decision that can lead to the happiness and peaceful life you have always wanted. If you decide to use counseling in your recovery plan from your anger, the worst that can happen is that you don't like it, and you can leave any time you choose. On the other hand, if you do give counseling an honest chance, you may find that your anger and your painful past might become a thing of the past and you help transform into the peaceful and loving person you were always meant to be.

**TIME TO TAKE ACTION**

1. Having your own safe person to talk to is a crucial step away from the angry life you have been living. Be willing to take this step.

2. Invite family and members or friends you trust to help you find someone you can be comfortable enough to open up to. Refer to the "7 Keys to Selecting Your Professional Counselor" on page 147 to help you with the process.

3. Make an initial appointment for a consultation with the counselor you select.

4. If you feel comfortable enough, you can take someone you trust to the first session. They will help you provide more background and details about your concerns to your counselor.

5. If all goes well in the first session, make an appointment for the second session that day. The first two sessions are crucial in getting the process started.

6. Journal about your counseling sessions after each session. This gives you the opportunity to review what happened in your most recent session and can also set the stage for what needs to occur in your next session.

7. Initially, speaking to a counselor may feel difficult, but stick with it. Establishing your relationship with someone you trust and committing yourself to the work that needs to be done can set the stage for a happier way to think and feel, and a much more productive to way live your life.

 **DRIVING IT HOME**

When you are setting up your network to help you reduce your anger, never forget that this is your life you are talking about. It is essential to include in this network a professional counselor who is there for you, can understand what you are thinking and feeling, and knows how to take you through the treatment and eventual recovery process from your anger. You have the right to obtain the absolute best care available. Anger can make you feel ugly and broken. You are not. You are beautiful. Never forget that. It is time to feel good about yourself.

**YOUR DECLARATION IS**: *I will take a risk and trust someone so I can resolve my anger and be happy!*

 **ONWARD**

Consistent with all the books in The Fix Yourself Empowerment Series, as we move into the last few chapters, I like to provide you with an idea of what life will look like if you stick to the plan I have outlined for you. In the next chapter, I give you a glimpse of what life can look like with anger reduced.

CHAPTER 23

# Living With Less Anger: Navigating Your New World

*Since we only live once, we need to live right. Live without anger and learn to love.*

> **PROCESSES TO EMPLOY:** Brutal Honesty, I Over E, Present/Understand/Fix, Slowing Down Life's Pace, Internal Focus, Fact-Finding, Living in the Moment, Settling Past Issues, Risk-Taking, Life Inventory, Belief, Sustained Learning, Trust, Love

**IF YOU ARE LIVING WITH ANGER,** it may have been part of your life for a long time. You may have been physically predisposed to conditions like neurotransmitter imbalance, a thyroid issue, or some other hormonal imbalance. You may have been raised in a family environment where anger was routinely expressed. You may not have experienced a different way to live, and being raised in that setting provided you with a template for the angry way you would live your life.

If you never understood that there is a more productive way to live, the idea of living without anger can feel a bit threatening. Of more importance, you might have no idea what you might be working for when it comes to reducing or removing anger from your life. Sometimes, it is difficult to attempt to make changes in your life when you are not sure what that will look like. I will use a step-by-step life-changing example as I begin to define what a world with reduced anger might look like.

Before I do that, it is important to define the angry and anger-free ways of living. An "angry life" is one where *your thoughts, feelings, and behaviors are anger-based, aggressive, defensive, retaliatory, critical, and volatile.* A life not controlled by anger *is one where your thoughts, feelings, and behaviors are warm, compassionate, communicative, understanding, peaceful, and loving (most of the time).* Once again, no one is completely anger-free. That is why I included the words "most of the time" in the definition.

## COMPARISON OF AN ANGRY LIFE VERSUS A LIFE WITH REDUCED ANGER

| Many Angry Thoughts | Reduced Anger Thoughts |
| --- | --- |
| Intense Emotions | Stable Emotions |
| Physical Stress | Is More Relaxed |
| Revengeful | Forgives Easily |
| Quick Reactor | Thinks Before Reacting |
| Is Condescending | Treats Others Equally |
| Blames Others | Holds Self Accountable |
| Indifferent Toward Others | Compassionate |
| Disrespects Others | Respects Others |
| Difficult to Talk to | Easy to Talk to |
| Cold and Standoffish to Others | Warm to Others |
| Complains Often | Easy to satisfy |
| Difficult Time Forgiving | Forgives Freely |
| Holds on to Past Pain | Lets Go of the Past |
| Difficult Time Taking Advice | Willing to Take Advice |
| Can Be Hostile | Is Peaceful |
| More Cold-Hearted | Loving |
| Often Unhappy | Usually Happy |

As you can see, the traits listed on the left side of the table represent a person who is dealing with anger in their life, and both displays and experiences the pain and unhappiness that is the product of an angry style of life. The right side of the table illustrates what it is like to have anger significantly reduced in one's life. Here, we see a person who is happier with themselves and displays a more loving approach toward other people. To continue to illustrate what your life can look like when you reduce anger's influence, I will provide you with that step-by-step life-changing example of a person living with anger and how by getting help for his problem, he begins to live a life that is more peaceful, happy, and loving.

## FROM ANGER TO PEACE: THE HEALING OF JACOB
### Part 1—In the Clutches

Jacob is a thirty-one-year-old business owner. He is the proprietor of South St. Glass and has three employees. Jacob has been married for seven years and has twin daughters who are three years old. He and his wife, Frances, have been married for nine years.

Jacob comes from an intense family background. His father is a recovering alcoholic, and his mother is a victim of child abuse. Jacob is the oldest of three boys, and all of them have had problems with anger. His older brother served three years in prison for aggravated assault, and his younger brother has had a DUI and often displays volatile anger.

Jacob is a loving father and a loyal husband. However, he is prone to angry outbursts. On one occasion, Frances called other family members to help her deal with Jacob, who was struggling with some business concerns, drank just a bit too much, and became more aggressive with her. There was no physical violence, but he was making angry overtures. Two weeks ago, Jacob had another angry outburst, and this time, he pushed Frances. After several years of putting up with his volatile anger, she has had enough. She informed Jacob that she was not going to subject herself or the girls to continue living in this type of environment. She wants a separation.

Though she has not taken any legal action, Frances is now living with her parents ten miles from their home. She informed Jacob that unless he gets help for his anger, she could no longer live with him. She has consulted an attorney, knows what her rights and responsibilities are, and has left the matter in Jacob's hands. Jacob will either do something to reduce his anger, or he may lose his family. Jacob feels as though he is a good man and defends himself by saying he is carrying most of the family's financial burden and that business has taken a dip since the pandemic. There is more to the problem, and Jacob has a decision to make.

Jacob's first decision was to promise his wife that he would no longer be violent. He told her that he understands his reasons for getting angry and knows that coming from a family where angry expressions were commonplace, he learned to do things the wrong way. Frances does agree that he is a good man, and for the most part, he treats her very well. She knows she is a good provider and a loving father. On the other hand, Frances can no longer be walking on eggshells, wondering what kind of damage is being done to their children.

Jacob has promised these kinds of things after previous angry outbursts, and Frances is now experienced enough to understand that he will keep his anger under control for a short time. She also knows that it will not take long for something to trigger Jacob's anger, and then things could get ugly. Frances has contacted a counselor and has attended two sessions with her. She understands that she must make a stand and that she can no longer allow Jacob to make excuses for his anger. She is taking her therapist's advice and has told Jacob that he must involve himself in a counseling program, or she will not entertain any future return home.

Frances informed Jacob of her decision, and this time, she is not backing down. She and her counselor are working on her boundaries and what she must do to defend them. She is unwilling to give Jacob another chance until he can understand what is causing his anger and learn other methods of dealing with it. She made it clear to him that her priorities are their daughters and pointed out that he, himself, coming from an anger-based home, learned how to be angry. She has no intention of subjecting her daughters to that kind of life. Jacob has the most important decision of his life ahead of him.

Initially, this was just another trigger to spark Jacob's anger. Having no other options than anger available to him at this point in his life, he reacted by telling her that it was her fault, he would never do this to her, and she was breaking up the family. On two occasions, after drinking a bit too much, he was sending her angry texts, and accusing her of being a homewrecker. Jacob was always able to manipulate Frances by doing this. He would make her feel guilty, and she would give him another chance. This time was different. She told him that if there was another angry text with more accusations, she would file for divorce. She also gave him a time limit for him to get himself into a counseling program.

Jacob has two choices that are available to him. He could do as his wife demands and contact the counselor, or he could continue being angry, lose his wife and children, half of what he owns, and pay spousal and child support. Jacob has a close friend who has been trying to help him. Jacob and Martin have been friends since childhood, and Martin has tried to help him address his anger several times in the past. This time, Martin was less understanding of Jacob's position and strongly advised his best friend to contact the counselor. Martin had some personal issues a few years back and gave Jacob the name and telephone number of his counselor.

Since the important people in Jacob's life were all telling him the same thing, and Jacob could now see how much he was going to lose, he decided to call the counselor. He said he would do this at his earliest opportunity. After two weeks, Frances called and asked if Jacob scheduled his first session. He said he was busy, and he was going to do it that weekend. Frances responded by saying, "Do it today or we are done." Backed into a corner, and with no way out, Jacob's procrastination strategy ended abruptly, and he scheduled the appointment with Dr. Baxter.

# FROM ANGER TO PEACE: THE HEALING OF JACOB
## Part 2—Recovery

Jacob canceled his first session with Dr. Baxter. He told him that something had come up at work and that he would call him back to reschedule. A week passed and Jacob did not reschedule. When Frances called to see how things were going, Jacob told her that he was enrolled in the counseling program. He failed to mention that he had not gone yet. Frances was expecting this and asked Jacob if she could come to his next appointment. Jacob knew exactly what she was doing, called Dr. Baxter, and rescheduled his appointment. Later that week, he attended his first counseling session.

In the first session, Dr. Baxter spent most of the session asking questions and writing things down. Much of what he asked was about Jacob's family history. There was some attention directed toward what was occurring in his life presently, but the focus seemed to be on these more formative years. Before making a second appointment, Dr. Baxter asked Jacob to make an appointment with his primary care physician and have a physical evaluation with blood analysis scheduled. He asked Jacob to call him back later that day to tell him when he was seeing his doctor. He also made it clear to Jacob that he knew he was procrastinating and wanted Jacob to understand that he was unwilling to move forward without a serious commitment from Jacob.

Jacob made and attended the appointment with his primary care physician. The doctor knew Jacob's family history and provided Jacob with a prescription for his blood analysis. On Dr. Baxter's *strong* advice, Jacob went for his blood test that day. A week later, test results were back, and a second appointment was scheduled with Dr. Baxter. There were two concerning results from the blood analysis. Jacob was suffering from high blood pressure, and his primary care physician gave him a prescription for a medicine to help with this. Also, his thyroid gland was a bit overactive, but his numbers did not lie outside of the normal parameters. This would be watched, but no treatment was immediately prescribed.

In Jacob's second session with Dr. Baxter, they discussed the physical results, and there was more attention given to his family life. At the end of the session, Dr. Baxter gave Jacob his initial findings. Jacob was astounded to see that he was using four different types of anger.

Physiological anger: Since the thyroid showed some significance, and high blood pressure was also involved, Dr. Baxter explained that these provided a physical undercurrent that was always there and kept Jacob primed for angry outbursts. Also, he explained that since there are no tests to determine neurotransmitter imbalance, he wanted to take a deeper look at this. There is a history of depression and anxiety on both the maternal and paternal sides of Jacob's family going back several generations. This could also be a contributing factor to his angry outburst, and considering the generational factor, neurotransmitter imbalance could be an underlying issue. Again, this was something they would watch. If things didn't improve, the possibility of medication could be indicated.

Verbal anger: Jacobs's angry displays typically begin with a change in the way he expresses himself verbally. He becomes critical, accuses other people, curses more, and attacks with an intent to hurt. This is the way Jacob's parents dealt with all three of their sons, and it is what Jacob learned to do. That would have to change.

Reactive anger: Almost every time Jacob displays anger, it is in reaction to something that happens. It could be at work, with friends, or at home. The venue doesn't seem to matter. When something happens, he quickly reacts, and his anger progresses from verbal outbursts to physical displays. He does not hurt other people, but he usually throws or breaks inanimate objects during these episodes.

Volatile anger: When Jacob becomes angry, he can go from a disposition that seems calm and rational to one that becomes quickly irate, irrational, and confronting. This can happen in a matter of seconds, usually lasts a few minutes, and then he begins to regain his composure. Once again, this behavior was displayed in his childhood, particularly by his father, and adopted as a way of living by Jacob and both his siblings.

A third session was scheduled, and Dr. Baxter told Jacob that at the end of the session, he would outline the treatment plan that would help him reduce the use of anger in his life. He also asked that Frances be part of that session. He was not willing to begin any type of marriage or couples counseling yet, but he did want Frances to understand the types of anger Jacob was dealing with, where it came from, and what he needed to do to address the problem. Frances could make up her mind about what she wanted to do based on Jacob's willingness to continue his counseling with Dr. Baxter and to follow through with the treatment plan.

In the third session, Dr. Baxter gave Frances the information she needed and answered her questions. Then, he presented the treatment program for Jacob. For one month, Dr. Baxter wanted Jacob to attend one individual counseling session per week with him, and an anger-management group that he runs with other men every week. Jacob thought this was a bit much, but agreed to it. He didn't want to do anything that would jeopardize a reunion with his family.

As the weeks progressed, Jacob and Dr. Baxter met individually. They addressed issues related to the undercurrents of anger in Jacob's life. Most of them came directly from his family. His father's drinking, and what doctor Baxter described as his mother's probable bipolar condition were important themes in his early development. His father, at times, physically abused the boys, and Jacob was bullied in junior high school. He responded by becoming a bully, if only for his desperate need for self-defense. Jacob was beginning to see the correlation between how he was treated during adolescence and how that developed into his angry disposition.

Jacob was also beginning to see how his anger was masking

some fear and insecurity, and how he used it to keep other people from getting too close. He began to see that a bit more anger was displayed following emotionally intimate times with Frances. Dr. Baxter explained how when Frances got too close, Jacob felt vulnerable and used anger to reestablish a safe distance.

In the group setting, Jacob was seeing other men open up, and he began to do the same. He saw that these other men had many of the same problems growing up that he did. It was a group of eight men at different stages in their treatment with Dr. Baxter. Jacob was seeing how other men were allowing themselves to be a bit vulnerable, and how the support of the group made doing so safe and provided invaluable information regarding how to live life without using so much anger. With the men in the group being at different stages of treatment, Jacob was able to see how some were in the initial stages of the program while others were farther along––that the program works. Their self-reports showed him how the program was working and how it might look several months down the road.

After three months, Dr. Baxter contacted Frances to say that it would be a good time to do couples counseling every other week. This would provide Jacob and Frances with the insights and tools they needed to move forward in their marriage, while not sacrificing the individual work that still needed to be done with Jacob. Frances agreed, and couples counseling began.

After three months of using this design, Dr. Baxter changed the design of the program. Jacob was making very good progress and hadn't had an angry episode in over four months. They would now attend couples counseling three weeks per month, and Jacob would have one session of individual counseling along with his group session. Jacob also had the option of scheduling additional individual appointments if necessary. Frances also decided to come back home. She discussed her boundaries and what she expected from Jacob.

Jacob and Frances continued with Dr. Baxter for another six months. They are now seeing him on an as-needed basis. Jacob continues to see Dr. Baxter monthly. The change in Jacob was significant and showed him that if a person is willing to face the problems they have in their life and commit the time it takes to understand where their anger came from, how it is affecting them and those around them, and how to make the necessary changes, life can become considerably more loving and peaceful.

## YOU CAN DO THIS

Anger has a way of masking so many other circumstances in your life. It can be difficult to understand what you are feeling and where those feelings are coming from. You didn't realize how desperate you were for help because anger produced the arrogance I discussed in Chapter 21. This told you that you were more powerful than you realistically were, that no one was going to tell you what to do, and that whatever was happening in your life was your business, and you would take care of it your way.

Learning how to express your pain so others could understand you was so important. Even in your most social moments, anger had you locked up inside yourself, and there was a devastating aloneness. It devastated you, and everyone close to you. Throughout this book, I have shown you the various types of anger and what anger can do to you. Jacob's story brings all that information to life. It should tell you that you are no different from anyone else. You are angry, and there are reasons for that anger.

You do not have to live as an angry person anymore. Jacob had to surrender his will, open himself up to one person, let that person help him, and change the way he was living his life. He was willing to do that. When he did, he began to remove anger from his world, and in the end, he didn't lose that world.

Keep this thought in mind. As far back as Chapter 1, I discussed how anger is a product of fear and insecurity. Sometimes, the unwillingness to get the type of help Jacob got comes from those fears and insecurities. You are afraid, and you are insecure. You don't know how to let someone in. Don't let that stop you. This is nothing more than you sitting down with one person who is trained to help you get past the pain that has kept you unhappy for so long. It can keep you from losing what is so important to you. Your time with your counselor is confidential, and you will finally have that one safe place that is yours and yours alone. When you think about it, that's exactly what's been missing for most of your life.

So, think of yourself as a worthy and valuable person. Be willing to invest the time it takes to become the happy person you can be. Remember, anger may feel like power, but it is the absence of power. Open up. Face the demons. Let someone help. Be the person you can be. Let nothing stop you. You are worth it.

## ⏱ TIME TO TAKE ACTION

1. Make a list of the angry thoughts you have. Share that list with a friend

2. Make a second list of the thoughts you have that are more positive. Share those with a friend.

3. Discuss the list with someone close to you, to determine if you are a more positive or angry thinker

4. Make that appointment with a counselor. Don't procrastinate. This is your fear keeping you away.

5. Use the list, and all other pertinent information about your anger to help your counselor assist you in putting together your program to reduce anger in your life. Follow the advice your counselor is giving you.

6. Use the information in this book, especially the parts that apply to the anger you are experiencing to help you establish a plan specific to your needs, one that will help you reduce anger in your life, and become a happier person period. Share it with your counselor.

7. It is a good idea to journal about what you are doing in counseling. This does not have to be a formal journal. Simply write down what you did in a counseling session, any thoughts you may have about it, and what you would like to talk to in the next session.

 **DRIVING IT HOME**

Anger does not have to be a life sentence. There are ways out of the pain that has been such an undercurrent in your life. The brave person isn't the one who faces things all by themselves to avoid opening up. Bravery is all about opening up to that one person who will help you change your life. While opening up to a counselor may activate the fight-or-flight response, don't run from this. Stand your ground. Face the demons. You are not alone anymore. That healthy, peaceful, life is waiting for you. You can do this!

**YOUR DECLARATION IS:** *I will let in someone who knows how to help me. Being open to help will change my life!*

 **ONWARD**

Like each book in The Fix Yourself Empowerment Series, this book concludes with a Good Housekeeping chapter. It is designed to help you understand that life is dynamic, will continue to change, and old nemeses can return, sometimes without notice. In the next chapter, I discuss what a repeat appearance of anger might look like and provide you with some practical ways to efficiently address that return visit.

# CHAPTER 24

## Good Housekeeping: Maintenance for the Long Haul

*Learn to identify your antagonists when they return. Know that you have the power to overcome them. You always will!*

**PROCESSES TO EMPLOY:** Brutal Honesty, I Over E, Present/Understand/Fix, Slowing Down Life's Pace, Internal Focus, Fact-Finding, Living in the Moment, Housekeeping, Settling Past Issues, System Maintenance

**MOST PEOPLE WHO DO THE WORK** to make desired changes a reality still experience brief periods of regression or reinvolvement in old habits. Many assume they have taken a step backward. When this happens, they can lose their focus. If productive plans for moving forward are compromised, some of those old negative feelings return, causing them to question whether they can even make lasting changes. In my counseling sessions with those going through the brief periods of reversal, I remind them of what I will now remind you:

*Your life is a fluid and dynamic enterprise.* It will continue to change, and the good and not-so-good will routinely enter your life. Anger ruled your life for so long, and you worked hard to loosen its grasp on your life. Things got better, and there is no doubt that this is a result of all the hard work you did. Hard work yields good results, and those results should be permanent. However, just because you did the work to make yourself healthier, wiser, and stronger does not mean that anger will not find its way back into your life.

Life does not stop just because you made improvements. Life is an ongoing affair, and the challenges inherent in living in an ever-changing world will continuously appear. It would be foolish to assume otherwise. This life is loaded with opportunities to interact with wonderful people and be part of pleasurable events, but it is also infested with anger-producing "toxins" and "demons" we would like to "strangle," especially when they return for an uninvited visit. This is when some intellectual and emotional housekeeping is in order.

Consider this example: You did all the work to remove anger from your life, and things are much better. Today, you are driving down the street, and someone pulls out in front of you. You slam on your brakes, but keep your composure and just look at the other person. Instead of an apology or at least an acknowledgment of wrongdoing, the window opens, their middle finger is in the air, and they're calling you a *%#@ing jerk. The old you would have quickly let your road rage engage, and the battle would be on. So, you didn't chase after this indignant fool, but you did return the hand gesture and the obscenities.

Now, your partner looks at you and says, "Really?" Though you didn't go into a full-scale angry tantrum, for a moment, you did let it get the best of you. This is where you need to take a step back and accept that you can make mistakes. Becoming agitated and lashing out are old autopilot ways of reacting to anger. Do not allow your anger to progress any further, apologize for creating stress in the other person's life, and return to the program you have been using to keep anger from dominating your life.

## RETURNING TO THE PROGRAM

Everyone takes a step backward from time to time, but that doesn't mean all the work you have done has been for nothing. That is far from the truth. There is a simple way to return to your program for healthy living. Here's how:

Assess the situation, understand where you went wrong, apologize quickly if you need to, and continue working with the program outlined in this book—period.

You are not perfect. You will have lapses in judgment, and at times, you will regress to your previous behavior. Sometimes you will just get tired and make a mistake. While your actions contained some negative energy, that does not mean you have not made progress or that your mistake might continue to move forward with you as your life continues. Everyone makes mistakes, and good sense tells us to quickly address those mistakes. Doing so allows us to return to what works for you and the positive energy that exists there.

When these situations occur, it is important to quickly admit what you did wrong, look at what you must do to make sure it doesn't happen again, and then keep taking the action steps provided throughout this book. This program is what helped you remove anger from your life, and it will help you get back on track when anger makes a return visit.

It is important to make sure that you do *not* use an excuse like, "Oh, everyone gets angry, and I probably will too." Never make excuses for your anger. Own what you have done, and start doing the things to help you remove angry reactions from your life. Know what you have done, try to understand why, be remorseful, make amends, and get back to doing things the right way.

Like all the books in The Fix Yourself Empowerment Series, you can use this book as a reference if you go off track. Since much of this behavior is connected to old autopilot ways of living, when you take that backward step, reread Part Three. This part provides the information you need to return to the program. Also, review any chapters that pertain to the types of anger you have. All that information combined will help you return to the plan to remove anger from your life.

## THE NEVER-ENDING STORY

Housekeeping is an ongoing state of affairs; a process of checks and balances never stops. All happy people must adjust, transition, and defend their gains on a routine basis. Know that if you remain committed to the processes you have been learning throughout this book, the external world becomes that much less oppressive. Housekeeping is one of those processes. When you use it, all return visitors are assigned to the new stronger version of you, and the negative and toxic invaders will perish there. Follow these steps and keep anger from overtaking your life:

### 7 Steps for Successful Housecleaning

1. Be ready for return visits from anger. They will inevitably come.
2. Identify the anger-producing situation or person.
3. Be honest with yourself about what is happening.
4. Slow down by doing breathing exercises. This will help you keep your emotions in check.
5. Gather all the necessary facts.
6. Based on the facts, develop a plan to address the problem, using your processes and your support people such as your counselor.
7. Execute your plan completely.

You made a brave decision when you decided to let someone in to help you work through the anger that has been affecting your life and the lives of those close to you. That may have been the most difficult part of learning how to live a life with reduced anger. Then you did all the work to settle old issues and learn how to think, feel, and behave without anger. Embracing the need for help, getting the help, and doing what you needed to do to remove anger from your life was the hard part. Think of the return visit as nothing more than a sidestep, and get right back to the steps that helped you change your life without looking back.

In the past, you had no program and no support system to back you up. You do now. Before taking the steps in this program, you likely felt alone, defeated, and without options. You are no longer alone. You have become stronger, and you have many options. Treat anger's return visit or any negative energy as something you took care of previously, and you will do so again.

Housekeeping is never an indication you have failed. Housekeeping is a wonderful reminder that you have the strength to, once again, remove anger from your world and continue living the loving, peaceful life you are creating.

 **TIME TO TAKE ACTION**

1. Address the return visitor with your intellect. There is no room for emotion here. Think; don't react.

2. Remember that this is a return visit. You fixed it the first time, so you know exactly what to do on the return visit. Use the processes and the action steps that apply to the return visit.

3. Never be surprised by return visitors. Some come from the outside, and some may be your own. Expect them to return. This will reduce a return visitor's shock value and your emotional response to it.

4. Accept the challenge with confidence and the understanding that you can address it—because you cane. Every successful housecleaning attempt increases your confidence.

 **DRIVING IT HOME**

While you can view housekeeping as another chore you must perform to keep anger from reentering your world, try not to think of it that way. Housekeeping is a wonderful process tool that is always available to you to keep you from regressing to old habits and experiencing the pain that can come from doing so. Use this process to remain anger-free as well as for any other improvements you make in your life. Become a person who routinely evaluates what you are doing and how you can do it better. Housekeeping reminds you how strong you are. It can be used not only to keep anger from entering your world but also as checks and balances that can be applied to every part of your life. Treat it as the gift it is, and keep your world positive, loving, and productive. Remember, you are a beautiful person. Be that person.

**YOUR DECLARATION IS:** *I will do my housekeeping every day of my life. I will keep my anger in check, and I will be happy!*

## *ONWARD!*

# Conclusion

**EVERYONE HAS A PAST. EVERYONE HAS PROBLEMS.** Everyone gets angry. You are no exception. There are many types of anger, and it is important to understand the facts about anger in general and about those that pertain directly to each kind of anger. Understanding your anger opens the door for a plan to help you reduce the anger and to learn how to live a life that is anger-free and happy.

Undercurrents are such an important part of understanding your personal anger history, how it makes you feel and behave today, and what you can do to move past those triggers. Anger causes thoughts, feelings, and behaviors that can jeopardize relationships, destroy families, involve you in the legal system, destroy your finances, and leave you lonely and broken.

No one needs to stay angry. There is always another way to deal with situations that produce anger. Being honest and admitting that you are angry is an important first step. Choosing to no longer blame others opens the door for the introspection and self-examination that is so necessary to understand where your anger is coming from.

Your anger will affect you physically, emotionally, intellectually, and spiritually. It can turn you into an arrogant person who is unwilling to take the advice of others and to make the changes to keep anger from destroying your life. All too often, it takes you to the brink of disaster before you understand how much you are going to lose.

Be willing to obtain the help you need to understand your anger, where it comes from, how it affects you, and how to formulate a plan to reduce its impact in your life. Get the help you need. Give yourself and those close to you the happy, peaceful life you all deserve. You are worth it, and you can do this!

# References

Ruggiero, Faust, M.S. 2023. *The Fix Your Anxiety Handbook*. Bangor, PA: FYHB Publications.

Ruggiero, Faust, M.S. 2023. *The Fix Your Depression Handbook*. Bangor, PA: FYHB Publications.

Ruggiero, Faust, M.S. 2019. *The Fix Yourself Handbook*. Bangor, PA: FYHB Publications.

# About the Author

Faust A. Ruggiero's professional career spans over forty years of diversified, cutting-edge counseling programs in pursuit of professional excellence and personal life enhancement. He is a published research author, clinical trainer, and therapist with experience in clinics for deaf children, prisons, nursing homes, substance abuse centers, inpatient facilities, and major national and international corporations. He has served as the president of the Community Psychological Center in Bangor, Pennsylvania, in which capacity he developed the Process Way of Life counseling program, presented as a formal text in *The Fix Yourself Handbook*.

Upon graduating from Mansfield University in 1977, he enrolled in the graduate psychology program at Illinois State University with a dual major in clinical and developmental psychology and a minor in research. He assisted in the publication of several research articles, including his thesis, "The Effects of Prosocial and Antisocial Television Programs on the Cognitions of Children."

Upon leaving graduate school in 1979, Mr. Ruggiero worked with Antoinette Goffredo to provide counseling services and psychological intervention to adolescent deaf children. He worked with Ms. Goffredo to develop a behavioral management program for profoundly deaf children with residual hearing.

In 1982, he accepted a position with the Lehigh Valley Alcohol Counseling Center. There, he provided individual counseling services to clientele suffering from alcohol abuse and addiction, including the twelve-step recovery process and family and intervention services. There, Mr. Ruggiero developed a Phase 2 counseling program for individuals convicted of drunk-driving offenses.

In 1984, he accepted a treatment position at Northampton County Prison, where he provided psychological and substance abuse intake and counseling services to inmates. He coordinated all substance abuse and program development services for inmates. In 1986, he obtained his certification in substance abuse treatment in the state of Pennsylvania.

In 1989, Mr. Ruggiero left Northampton County prison to pursue his endeavors at the Community Psychological Center full-time. As President of the Community Psychological Center, Mr. Ruggiero continued to provide services to individuals, families, those suffering from substance abuse, abused women and women in transition, as well as couples and marriage counseling, and counseling for veterans, law enforcement, and other first responders. In 1990, he began providing employee assistance programs to corporations in the state of Pennsylvania. Since then, he has been nationally and internationally recognized for his business approaches focused on strengthening corporate administrators and their workforces. In 1994, Mr. Ruggiero accepted an invitation to become a trainer for the Department of Health in Pennsylvania.

Following several years of experimentation with various therapeutic approaches that could be applied to clients individually and in families, social relationships, and business and corporate settings, Mr. Ruggiero developed and employed the Process Way of Life Counseling Program. The program consists of over fifty internal human processes, which can be accessed and developed to help clients address the various conditions affecting their lives. The program was developed, rigorously researched and tested, and revised into the approach he is presently uses at the Community Psychological Center.

In the summer of 2016, Mr. Ruggiero began to develop The Fix Yourself Empowerment Series based on the Process Life

Program to help readers address the difficult situations in their lives. The award-winning *The Fix Yourself Handbook* was completed in December 2019. He has appeared on television, radio shows, and podcasts both national and international to discuss the Process Way of Life. His radio show "Fix It With Faust" debuted in June 2021. On June 8, 2023, the second installment in The Fix Yourself Empowerment Series, *The Fix Your Anxiety Handbook*, was published. It is also an award-winning publication. In December 2003, *The Fix Your Depression Handbook* was published. It is the third book in the series. The *Fix Your Anger Handbook*, the series' fourth book, was published in May 2024.

www.ingramcontent.com/pod-product-compliance
Lightning Source LLC
Chambersburg PA
CBHW072152070526
44585CB00015B/1107